# SMALL BARN PLANS

## FOR OWNER-BUILDERS

*Your step-by-step guide to saving thousands on your new barn – plus complete construction plans for 12 best-selling barn designs*

***by* Craig Wallin**

Homestead Design
Port Townsend Washington 98368

***by* Craig Wallin**

*Published by:*
Homestead Design, Inc.
Post Office Box 2010
Port Townsend, WA 98368 U.S.A.
www.homesteaddesign.com


Library of Congress Control Number: 2002107071
ISBN 0-933239-37-8



Disclaimer - This book is provided as a helpful guide for owner-builders. It is sold with the understanding that the author and publisher are not providing legal, accounting or other professional services. Every effort has been made to verify the information in this book. However, there may be mistakes. Therefore, this book should be used as a general guide, and any information double-checked.

The information and plans in this book are presented for educational purposes only, and should not be used to construct a building without first consulting with local design or building professionals. They can assist you in making sure the information and plans are suitable for your specific building site, and the requirements of your local building codes and ordinances. This will help insure that your building will be safe and sound.

The purpose of this book is to educate and inform the readers. The author and the publisher shall have neither liability nor responsibility to any person or entity with respect to any loss or damages caused, or alleged to have been caused, directly or indirectly, by the information contained in this book. If you do not wish to be bound by the above, you may return this book to the publisher for a refund.

# Contents

# Acknowledgements

Thanks to the many people who helped with this book by contributing designs, ideas and suggestions. A special thanks goes to Jeanne Wallin, a residential designer and partner in Homestead Design, for her design work. Jerry Smith's barn renderings capture the special quality of each barn. Donald J. Berg, A.I.A. shared many ideas and several of his expandable "American Wood" designs. Sandy Hershelman's editorial efforts improved the text, and appreciation goes to Ruth Marcus for the outstanding book design and production.

Thanks also to the hundreds of owner-builders who shared their experiences, good and bad, with me over the years. Their enthusiasm, perseverance and willingness to learn are the real inspiration for this book.

Thanks to the following for providing illustrations or photos: American Wood Council, Robert Biffle, Country Manufacturing, Midwest Plan Service-U.S.D.A., National Manufacturing, and the Northeast Regional Agricultural Engineering Service at Cornell University.

# Introduction

In the early days of America, farming was as interwoven with everyday life as driving a car is today. Those farmers of past centuries lived in an age when a barn was a necessary and integral part of life. Then, the barn functioned as a shelter for livestock as well as a place to store feed and farm implements out of the weather.

Today, most of us are not full-time farmers—and barns have changed accordingly. Gone are the traditional threshing floors and granaries. They've been replaced by an amazing variety of non-traditional uses. Barns now shelter artist's studios, emus, ostriches and pot-bellied pigs, craft shops, workshops, and much more. That's the reason for this book. Barns are not just for cows anymore!

For more than 20 years, Homestead Design has been designing (and building) structures to fit the changing needs of America's population.
In addition to providing plans for professional builders and contractors, we've been supplying plans to more and more owner-builders. These "weekend builders" look forward to a change from their weekday office job, and enjoy the satisfaction that comes from completing a challenging construction project.

In addition, most of our customers look forward to saving a sizeable chunk of money by doing part or all of the work themselves. Since as much as 50 percent of the cost of a building is often labor and overhead, the savings to an owner-builder can be substantial. In this book, you'll learn how to save money on your building project by "working smarter, not harder". Many of our customers report savings of up to 25 percent without even lifting a hammer or a paint-brush!

Who should tackle a building project of this size? If you're a do-it-yourselfer with modest carpentry skills and a willingness to learn, stretch those skills and build it better yourself. If you're not quite ready for a single-handed building project of this size, team up with an experienced carpenter or builder and learn as you save. When you're done, you'll have a building you can be proud of!

Unlike most other books about barn building, this book's focus is on the pre-construction part of building, where most owner-builders lack experience—and where it's also possible to save a pile of money. As experienced builders know, there's a lot of planning and design work to do before the actual ground-breaking—work that can make the building project much easier, and the completed project a joy to use. Using the money-saving tips and techniques in this book, you'll end up with a more affordable building, or more building for the same dollars. Either way, you win!

Even if you plan to hire professionals to do most of the work, you'll still find project management ideas in this book to help you complete your building on time and on budget. We'll take you through the entire planning process, starting with how to choose a design that's right for your needs and budget.

Starting with your own "wish list" plus a checklist of other building requirements, you'll learn how to design a barn that works for you, and how to "site" the building to avoid problems. You'll also learn how to adapt one of the professional building plans included in this book to your requirements.

I've worked closely with hundreds of owner-builders during the last 20 years. I've found the majority of them prefer to start with a "stock" plan and modify it to suit their needs. Of course, every plan needs a few changes to make it the "perfect" plan for you. To be honest, I don't think anyone I know has built a stock plan exactly as drawn. They need to be adapted to a building site, or a window needs to be moved to the sunny side, or " I love the design, but let's shorten it by eight feet to meet the budget!"

In Chapter 2, you'll learn how to customize a stock plan to fit your needs, your building site, and your budget. You'll learn some design "rules of thumb" to ensure the finished building is functional and pleasing to the eye.

Years ago, when things were simpler, it was actually possible to build without permits or permission from the local authorities. Today, unfortunately, a typical building project takes longer to get through the permitting process than to actually build!

In Chapters 4 and 5 you'll learn how to estimate building costs and schedule the building process so workers and materials are at your project when you need them there. In Chapters 6 and 7, you'll learn building code basics, how to obtain permits and work with local building and zoning officials with a minimum of hassle.

Since working with subcontractors is an essential part of the building process, you'll learn how to manage those wonderful folks known in the trade as "subs". Then, because it's always easier—and cheaper—to learn from someone else's mistakes, we'll cover a few of the more common mistakes I've seen owner-builders make, and tell you how to avoid most of them.

You'll find complete construction plans for several small barns in Chapters 10, 11 and 12. I've chosen the plans that have been the most popular with owner-builders through the years, and arranged them by exterior shape and size. In addition, you'll find suggested design variations to allow you to customize a plan to meet your needs, whether you're housing hogs or humans.

You'll probably find parts of several designs that fit your needs. Feel free to combine ideas, move windows or doors, and experiment with the spaces. The purpose of this book, after all, is to encourage you to experiment and consider a multitude of possibilities for what, I hope, will become your personalized building design.

Chapters 13 and 14 include valuable resources for owner-builders, including several useful construction forms, additional building resources such as manufacturers of barn components and even a source for free barn plans!

One of the best resources for owner-builders is not listed in this book. It's the local builders and tradespeople who live in your town. Don't be afraid to ask questions—most professionals are happy to help out a novice builder.

As you build your perfect barn, don't forget to take the time to enjoy your work and have fun!

# How much can an owner-builder save?

Using the information in this book can help you save from 15 to 40 percent on your new barn. Whether you choose to be "hands on" and do most of the work yourself, or simply manage the building project, there are lots of ways to save thousands of dollars. Here are the major ways:

| Builder markup and profit | 20% to 40% |
|---|---|
| Savings on materials | Up to 10% |
| Doing work yourself | Up to 20% |
| Competitive bidding | 10% to 20% |

Let's take a closer look at these four categories to learn exactly how you, too, can achieve similar savings.

## Builder markup and profit

Contracting is simply coordinating the work of subcontractors and managing the building process so that it flows smoothly. The cost of doing business, usually called "overhead" or "markup" for most small contractors, runs around 25 to 30 percent. This covers everything from insurance for employees to buying and maintaining trucks, tools and equipment. To stay in business, a contractor has to cover these costs or he'll go under. You, on the other hand, will have far lower overhead for your building project, and can pocket the savings.

Contractors also add a profit margin to their bid, which is typically 10 to 15 percent. Some builders add a profit markup to everything, including materials and labor, while others price out the materials at cost. Either way, as the owner-builder, you can eliminate the profit markup too, and save another 10 to 15 percent by acting as your own contractor.

## Savings on materials

Since materials amount to half the total cost for a typical barn, it pays to look for ways to trim the cost of those materials. Here are eight time-tested ways.

1. Always get three bids on materials. You'll likely find a spread of 6 to 10 percent from low to high bidder. Lumberyards that specialize in "contractor

sales" will be very competitive on a whole building package. You don't have to be a contractor to get the best prices either, just be willing to have your materials package be delivered in one to three truckloads and pay promptly.

2. Lumber prices tend to be seasonal, so you can often save 20 to 30 percent by buying your framing package "off-season". You'll notice this particularly with plywood and OSB (Oriented Strand Board), which can often creep up as much as 30 to 40 percent from the slow winter season to the busy spring and summer building season.

3. Buy on sale. Just like shopping for groceries or TVs, many building products will go on sale at the major home centers. If it's not on sale, ask "When is this going on sale?" It costs nothing to ask.

4. The national home centers, such as Home Depot and Lowes, typically take 10 percent off your first purchase when you open an account with them. Compare prices first, and then open that account with the purchase of your complete framing package. One of our customers was able to save $850 using this technique. The same national chains will often offer to take 5-10 percent off a competitor's price, which can result in additional savings for you if you've already comparison shopped.

5. Buy at the "boneyard". Window and door manufacturers, and dealers, have a steady supply of returned windows that were mistakes. Six inches too tall, or three inches too narrow, and it's off to the boneyard! If you can visit a boneyard before framing starts, it's possible to change opening sizes to accommodate your boneyard deals. And you will get deals—prices are typically ten to fifty cents on the dollar!

6. Buy salvaged building materials. Most towns have a salvage dealer, or two, who offer building materials at substantial discounts. A recent visit to our local dealer found new hardwood flooring at 50 percent off retail, and recycled fir beams at 40 percent off new prices. Bill Gates, who doesn't have to budget, used recycled fir beams for his new $50 million dollar house.

7. Reduce scrap by using standard sizes. I once visited a job site where the scrap pile was huge. I asked the contractor why it was so big. Turns out, the owner designed the house with odd, not even, dimensions, so every wall generated more scrap. Keep this in mind when you design your new barn. Lumber comes in multiples of two feet (10 feet, 16 feet, etc.). Plywood, and other sheathing, is widely available in four-by-eight foot sheets. Take advantage of these common sizes when planning your building project, or you'll end up with lots of very expensive firewood.

8. Buy your own materials. Since most contractors add a markup to their cost of materials, you'll generally save the 10 to 15 percent markup if you buy the materials yourself. Your savings can be substantial. The cost of the framing package for a typical barn can be $10,000. If you buy direct from the lumberyard or home center with the best bid, you'll save the $1,000 to $1,500 contractor markup.

## Doing the work yourself

For some owner-builders, saving money is the most important reason to get involved in the actual construction of their new barn. For others, it's the feeling of accomplishment after completing a substantial building project.

Whatever your reasons, you'll need to take an objective look at your construction skills and confidence levels with a particular job, such as pouring a foundation or doing electrical work. If you lack the skills and knowledge in an area, you'd be wise to call a pro.

Most of the owner-builders I've worked with choose a compromise. They do some, but not all the work. Rather than trying to do it all, they hire a pro to do the foundation, so they start off "level and square". Many have found using a framing subcontractor can really speed up the process , at a reasonable cost. The framing for most small barns can be completed in a week or two.

Even if you "only" do all of the assorted jobs after the building shell is up, you can still save as much as 15 percent of the total cost.

## Competitive bidding

- **Rule #1 : Always get at least three bids.**
- **Rule #2 : Never forget Rule #1.**

I recently had a chat with a client who was convinced her Uncle Jerry, a general contractor, would give her a rock-bottom "kinfolks" price on her new barn. Fortunately, I was able to convince her that Uncle Jerry wouldn't need to know that she was getting two more bids, just to compare. Turns out Uncle Jerry was the high bidder—by 30 percent—and she saved more than $9,000 just by taking the time to get two more competitive bids.

In Chapter 8, I'll cover the bidding process in detail, but for now, remember that the normal "spread"—high to low—for residential bids ranges from 10 to 20 percent. So if you don't get multiple bids, you'll never know if the first bid was the highest or lowest!

# Barn Design Basics

The perfect barn for you is the one you planned and built! To help turn your dream barn into reality, let's look at the options available, so you can decide what works best for you.

The two most common methods are to design the barn from "scratch" yourself, and to adapt a "stock" plan. The first method can be a challenge, but not impossible. By using the barn designs shown in Chapters 10-12, you'll have actual construction drawings to refer to, and design guidelines to help.

The second, adapting an existing plan, is the method used by most people. It's generally easier, because you're not starting from scratch. There are hundreds of barn plans to choose from, as a starting point for your modifications. You may not find one that exactly fits your needs and building site, but in the pages that follow, you'll learn how to easily—and safely—modify a stock plan.

Even if you draw a floor plan that meets your needs, you may lack the technical skills or confidence to turn it into a set of "working drawings" necessary to get a permit or bids from contractors. An architect or building designer can do it all for you, but the cost may be more than you want to spend.

Fortunately for you, almost every community has a drafting course taught at either the high school or community college level. No, I'm not suggesting you enroll, although you could. For most of you who just want a barn, not a drafting certificate, you can contact the drafting instructor. Many of them draft plans as a sideline, as a teacher's salary can always use a boost. If the instructor is not interested, ask them for the name of their best student. You should then negotiate a fixed price for the plans, rather than an hourly rate.

## The real world

For most of us, there is a constant balancing act between what we want and what we can afford. Barns are no different. The average person's wish list for a "perfect" barn shrinks considerably when confronted with the reality of costs. Still, it's possible to juggle what you want, and what you can afford, in creative ways to give you more of what you want.

For example, a barn design that's expandable can grow to meet your wish list over time, as your budget allows. You can build a "bare bones" barn, and finish it as the money and time permit. In the pages that follow, you'll learn how to expand a barn design, so it not only gives you the extra space you need, but looks great too!

Now, let's get back to that "wish list". Make a list of what you plan to use the barn for—horses, a tractor, a workshop, or craft studio? How much space do you need to accommodate these uses? Be sure to measure any equipment you plan to store—height, width and length.

To help you, here are guidelines for stall sizes and storage requirements for common barn staples, such as hay. And don't forget, are the doors sized to move the stored equipment in and out?

| **Space Requirements for Animals** | |
|---|---|
| Cows | 30 square feet per head |
| | 100 square feet for calving pen |
| Sheep | 20 square feet for ewes |
| | 30 square feet for ewes & lambs |
| | 10 square feet for lambs |
| Hogs | 20 square feet each |
| | 40 square feet for sow & litter |
| Chickens | 4 square feet per bird |
| Turkeys | 6 square feet per bird |
| Breeder Turkeys | 10 square feet per bird |
| Ducks | 4 square feet per bird |
| Breeder Ducks | 8 square feet per bird |
| Geese | 4 square feet per bird |
| Breeder Geese | 8 square feet per bird |

| **Stall Sizes for Horses** | |
|---|---|
| Miniature Horse | 6 by 8 feet |
| Pony | 10 by 10 feet |
| Small Horse<br>Under 900 lbs. | 10 by 10 feet<br>or 10 by 12 feet |
| Riding Horse<br>900-1300 lbs. | 10 by 12 feet<br>12 by 12 feet (best) |
| Small Draft Horse | 12 by 14 feet<br>14 by 14 feet (best) |
| Large Draft Horse | 16 by 16 feet |

## Barn design for horses

Since so many barns are built to house horses, let's review the fundamentals of horse barn design. Designing a barn for your horses means starting with a "wish list" based on the number of horses you plan to house, and the additional space requirements, such as feed and bedding storage, a tack room, and an area for grooming. Most horse barns use a center aisle layout, with stalls on one or both sides of the aisle.

### *AISLES*

Aisles should be at least 10 feet wide, to allow room to turn a horse around or groom a horse on ties. A 12-foot wide aisle allows room to drive a full-size pick-up or a large tractor from one end of the barn to the other.

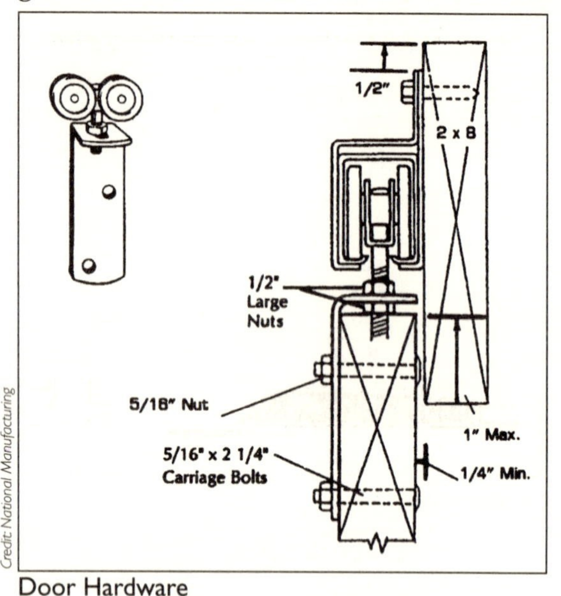

Door Hardware

Although the minimum headroom in aisles (and box stalls) is eight feet, 10 or even 11 feet is better, because the extra height allows a rearing horse room to move without hitting its head. It's easy to change the height of barn walls before you begin construction by simply increasing the wall heights on the plans to the desired height. If the aisle ceiling is less than 10 feet high, recess any light fixtures to protect them from horses.

### *AISLE DOORS*

Be sure to size the aisle doors for the largest equipment you plan to bring into the barn. Sliding doors are safer than swinging doors, especially in windy conditions or when leading a horse. If you plan a sliding door more than eight feet wide, split it into two parts that open at the center of the aisle, rather than at one side. This makes the door section lighter in weight and easier to open and close. Sources for sliding barn door hardware are listed in Chapter 14.

For low maintenance and durability, aisle floors are usually concrete, although you can pour the concrete floor later, if your barn building budget is tight. Asphalt is sometimes used, because the cost is lower, but it's not as durable as concrete.

### STALLS

The basic requirement for a box stall is that your horse has room to lie down, get up, and turn around without difficulty. The stall size chart gives the recommended sizes for stalls. Don't make the stalls larger than needed; you'll just waste bedding. For example, a 10 by 10 stall is 100 square feet, but a 12 by 12 stall is 144 square feet — and uses almost 50 percent more bedding.

One way to keep stall sizes flexible is to use a removable partition between two stalls. This allows you to provide a larger stall for foaling, or for housing a larger horse, when needed. You can fabricate a movable wood partition yourself or use pre-fab components from one of the suppliers listed in Chapter 14.

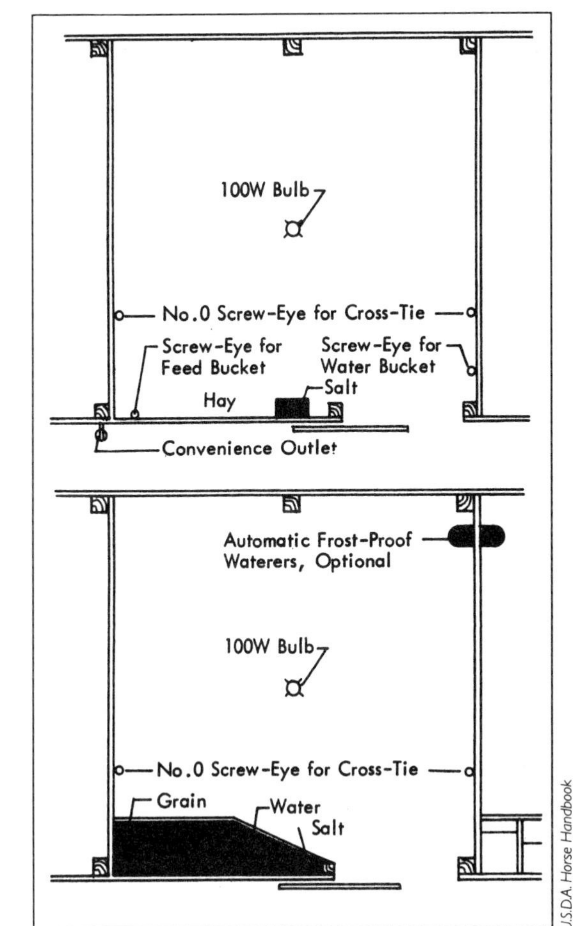


U.S.D.A. Horse Handbook

Sample stall layout

U.S.D.A. Horse Handbook

Stall door

### STALL DOORS

If your budget allows, provide two doors for every stall; one directly to the outside, and one to the aisle. A standard opening size is four feet, which allows ample room for both horses and a cleanup cart.

Dutch doors, with a separate hinge and latch for the top and bottom sections, are a good choice for exterior doors because you can open just the top to provide light and ventilation.

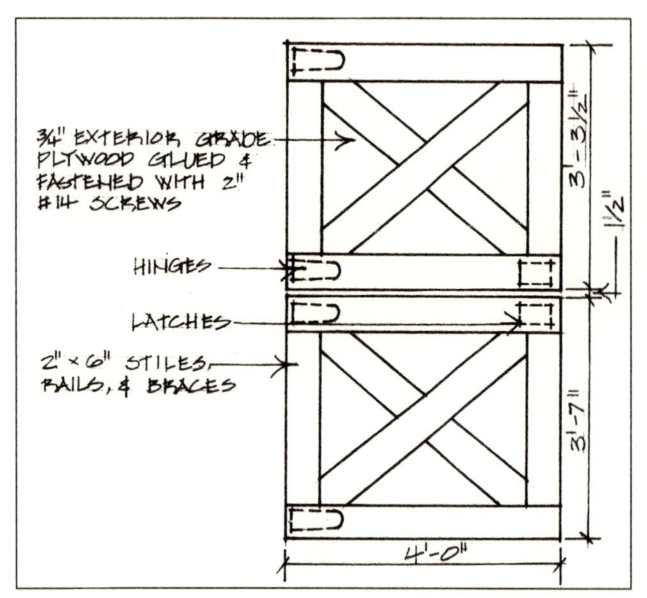

Dutch Door Detail

Sliding doors are preferred for the aisle side of stalls, because they take up less space and can be opened even if a horse is lying against it. A roller and guide on both sides of the door bottom will prevent a horse from getting a foot stuck between the door and wall. Another option, especially if your building budget is tight, is a metal stall guard in place of a door on the aisle side.

### *STALL WINDOWS*

Stall windows can provide light and ventilation for stalls, but must be protected from horses. Install heavy screening, such as one-to-two inch galvanized mesh, or a metal grill, to keep the horses away from the glass.

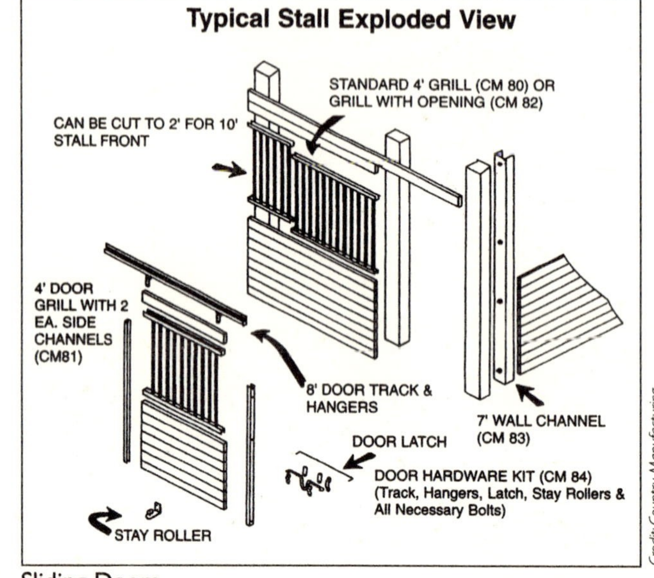

Sliding Doors

Credit: Country Manufacturing

### *STALL FLOORING*

The ideal stall flooring should provide a surface that's easy on your horses, easy to clean, and easy to maintain. For most barns, packed clay or stall mats over a concrete slab are the two floors of choice. Both should slope slightly—about two inches in 10 feet is enough to provide drainage, but not so much that it strains your horse's legs. A packed clay floor, while less expensive, requires more maintenance. A concrete slab, covered with a stall mat, costs more, but reduces maintenance.

### TACK STORAGE

If you're building a smaller barn, you may want to include as many stalls as possible, and just store your tack gear in a trunk. If space allows, however, it's good to provide a separate tack area. Here are a few features you might want to include in your tack room:

- Running water and a utility sink
- Counter/workbench for working on tack
- Electrical outlets for tools, coffee maker, etc.
- Saddle rack
- Storage cabinets for brushes, wraps, clippers, etc.
- Small "dorm size" refrigerator for vaccines and beverages

### FEED ROOM

For easy access, try to locate the feed room as close as possible to the stalls. Make sure the door and latch is horse-proof. Metal garbage cans are a good choice because they protect the feed from insects and rodents. An average 30-gallon can will hold about 100 pounds of feed.

The door to your feed room should be at least four feet wide to make it easy to carry bags of feed into the room. You'll need about 60-80 square feet of space in your feed room for the average two to six stall barn. If space is limited, think about combining the feed room and the tack room.

### HAY STORAGE

Whether you're cutting your own hay or buying a few bales at a time, you'll need a dry storage space that's convenient to the stalls. Here's how much space you'll need:

| | | |
|---|---|---|
| Loose hay | 4 pounds per cubic foot | 500 cubic feet per ton |
| Loosely baled hay | 6 pounds per cubic foot | 330 cubic feet per ton |
| Tightly baled hay | 12 pounds per cubic foot | 165 cubic feet per ton |
| Loose straw | 2-3 pounds per cubic foot | 660-1000 cubic feet per ton |
| Baled straw | 4-6 pounds per cubic foot | 330-500 cubic feet per ton |

As you can see from the chart, baled hay is heavy, so be sure the loft floor joists and beams are sized to handle the load. For example, hay bales stacked six feet high in the loft weigh about 70-75 pounds per square foot, almost twice the normal loading for a loft floor.

If you plan to use the loft area for hay storage, make sure to provide access for a hay bale conveyor for loading. Using tongue-and-groove plywood for the loft floor will help reduce dust.

Because of the fire hazard and the health hazards to horses created from airborne dust, many horse experts suggest storing hay and bedding in a separate building, or in an extra stall on the ground floor. For example, a 6-by-12-foot area will store 80 bales, enough to feed four horses for two months.

#### *VENTILATION*

Natural ventilation can be easily and inexpensively provided by installing screened vents in the eaves, and a continuous ridge vent, or a cupola, at the roof peak.

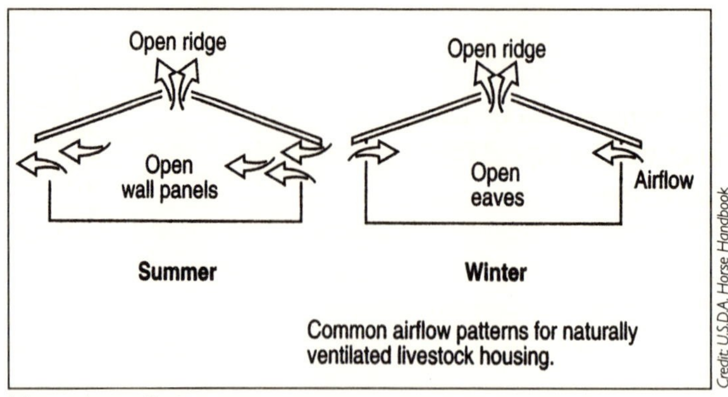

Natural ventilation

An exhaust ventilation system can supplement natural ventilation, when the temperature or humidity is high, by using a fan to force the air out of the barn. The fan should be located in the roof or high in a gable end wall, out of reach of any animals. The fan should have a capacity of 100 cubic feet per minute per horse. A variable speed control will allow you to reduce the airflow in cold weather. Add a thermostat, located at eye level, in the center of the barn, for automatic ventilation.

## How to modify a stock plan

Adapting a stock plan to fit your building site and meet your needs and budget is not difficult, as long as you follow some common-sense guidelines. Modifications usually fall into two categories:

***It's important, even with seemingly minor changes, to have a qualified building professional review your modifications to make sure they don't overload any part of the building.***

#### *SIMPLE CHANGES*

- Adding or moving windows or doors
- Moving interior non-bearing walls
- Changing the roof slope
- Adding a foot or two to exterior wall height

#### *MAJOR CHANGES*

- Adding a wing
- Adding a dormer
- Enlarging the building
- Changing from "stick-framing" to "pole-framing"

Simple changes are usually non-structural; that is they don't alter the structural integrity of the building. For example, moving a window or door to a new location is okay, as long as you also move the "header" beam, above the door or window opening, to the new location. A header provides support for the weight of the building above an opening. If the opening size for the window or door is increased, you'll need to provide a larger header beam,too.

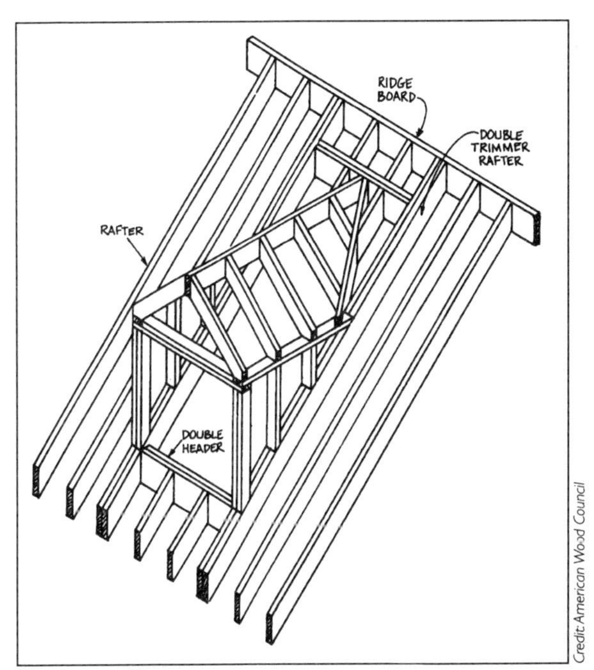


Credit: American Wood Council

Doghouse Dormer

Another potentially hazardous example would be using a loft that was designed for "normal" floor loads for hay storage, which requires a much stronger floor structure. It's not difficult to change the floor joists and beams on paper, but dangerous if you don't!

Most barns are designed to have a flexible interior, with few load-bearing structural walls. If you move any interior walls, make sure that they are non-bearing. A non-bearing wall is one that does not support any part of the building above it.

### *ADDING A DORMER — OR TWO*

Adding dormers can improve the appearance of a barn, as well as provide more useable space and light in a loft or attic. The two most common dormer styles are the "doghouse" dormer, and the shed dormer.

Because adding a dormer removes roof rafters and places additional loads and stress on the remaining rafters and ridge beam, make sure to check with a

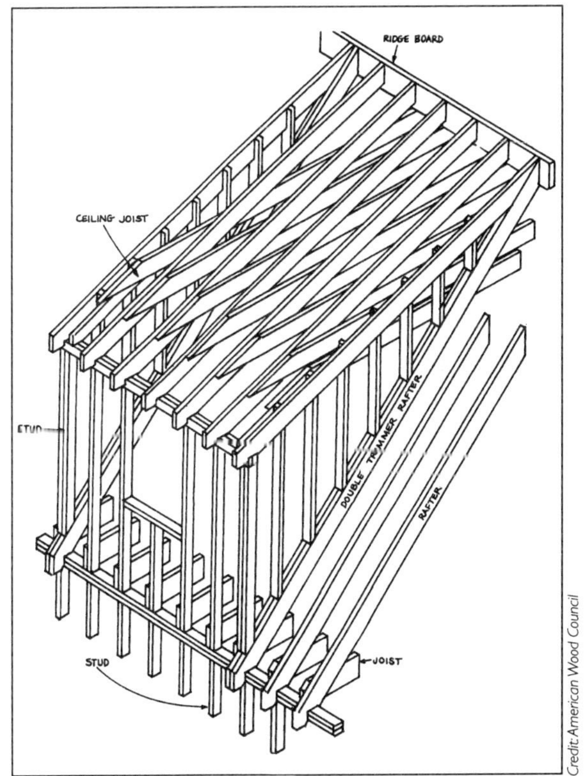


Credit: American Wood Council

Shed Dormer

local building professional to find out how to compensate for the extra loads. Often, with smaller dormers, it's simply a matter of doubling up the rafters on either side of the dormer.

Basic barn

### *ADDING A WING – OR TWO*

One of the easiest—and most affordable—ways to add space to a barn is to extend one or more wings from a "core" barn. Shed roofed wings have always been popular, as they are simple and easy to build. The Pilchuck barn, featured in Chapter 10 of this book, includes a shed-wing plan that increases the usable space by more than 60 percent. Adding two wings, one on each side, more than doubles the space, from 384 square feet for the core barn, to 864 square feet!

Barn with added wing

Architect Donald Berg has designed a remarkable collection of expandable small barns that uses a series of expansion wings and one core barn to provide up to 25 different plan variations for use as barns, workshops or garages. To see the whole series of "American Wood" barn designs, visit his web site, www.abetterplan.com.

Credit: Donald J. Berg, A.I.A.

Applewood barns

Credit: Donald J. Berg, A.I.A.

Chestnut horse barns

Walnut barns and garages

Maple garages and barns

### *ENLARGING A BARN PLAN*

If you've found a stock plan you like, but need a few extra feet to accommodate an extra stall or two, or your collection of Ferraris, consider the cut-and-paste technique.

Cut and paste works only when you stretch the length of a barn. (Changing the width of a building alters spans for joists and rafters, which requires re-calculating the structural loads and stresses on the structure and re-sizing components when required.)

Here's an example of cut and paste, using the "Austin" five-stall barn featured in Chapter 12. Let's assume you decide to add two more stalls than shown in the stock plan for the Austin.

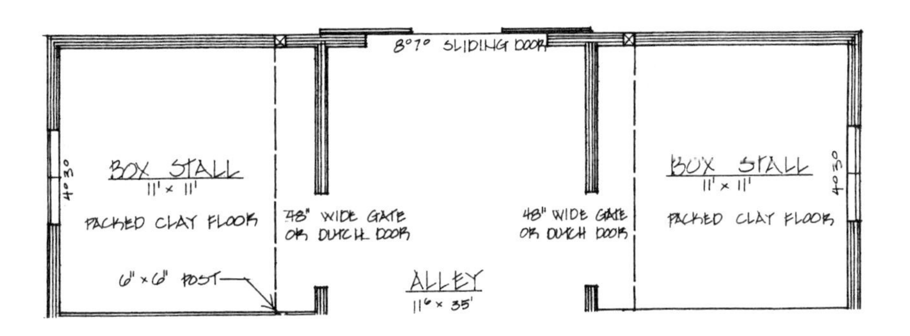


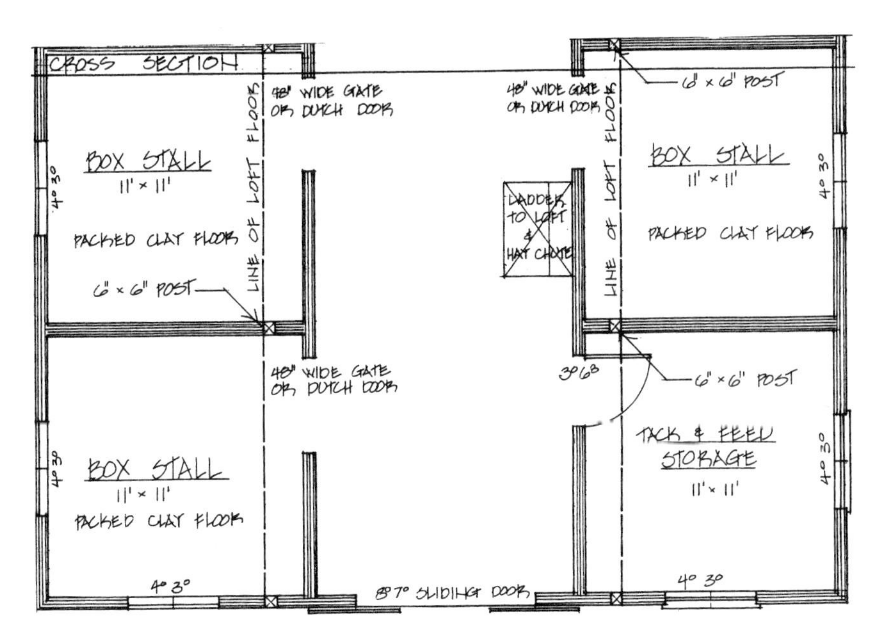


Original floor plan, with cut.

Simply make photocopies of the floor plan, cut out a 12-foot section, and add it to the existing floor plan. Presto! You've got a seven-stall barn! Now, do the same cut and paste to the exterior elevations, the foundation plan, and the loft floor and roof framing plan. Then, make copies of your new expanded plans. You'll also need to change the materials list to reflect the larger size of the barn.

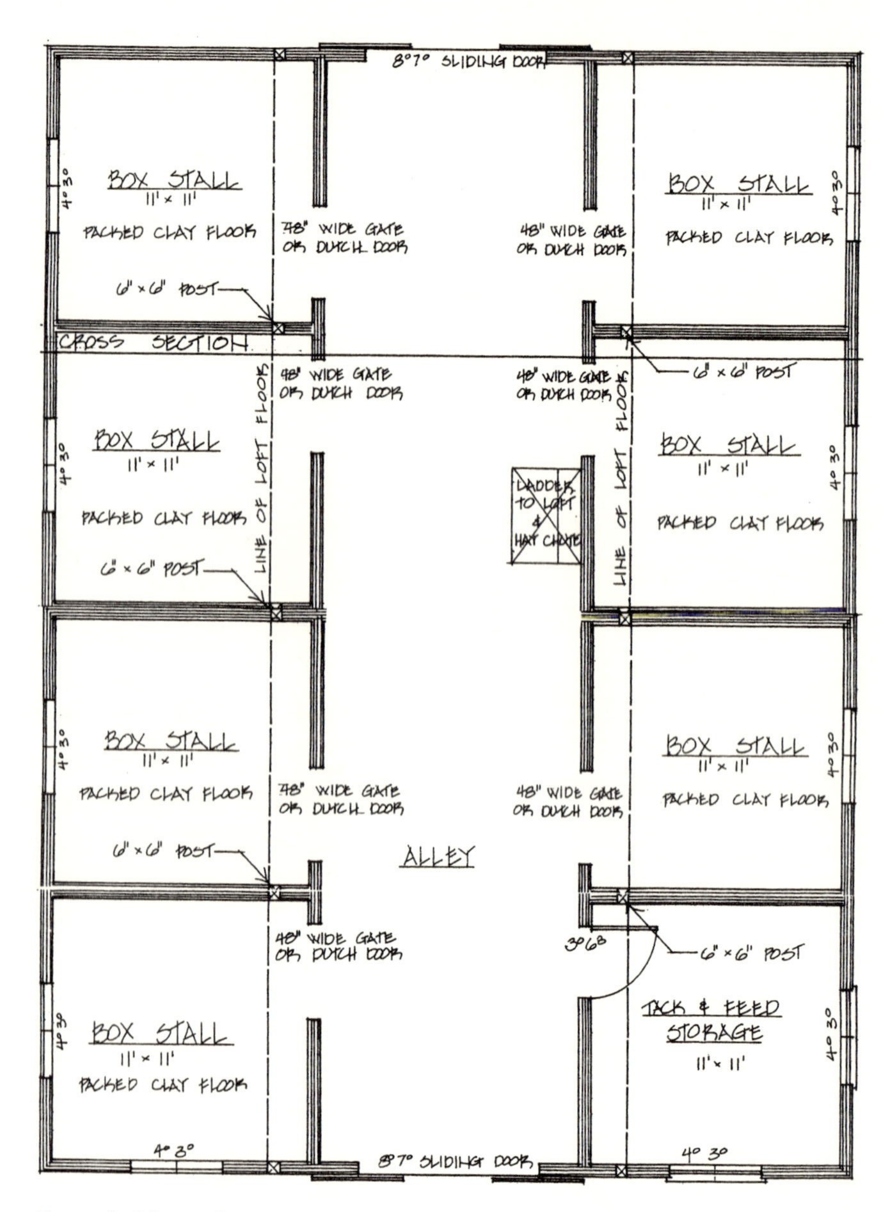


Expanded floor plan

### *CONVERTING TO POLE-FRAME CONSTRUCTION*

Pole buildings are popular because of their relative simplicity and lower cost, although they can cost the same as conventional stick-framing if the interior is finished. To adapt a stock barn plan that uses stick-frame construction (as is used in most house construction) to pole-frame construction, first read the "Post-Frame Building Handbook" (order number NRAES-1). Your local county extension agent should have a copy you can borrow, or you can order your own from the source listed in the appendix. Local builders who specialize in pole-frame buildings can be helpful also.

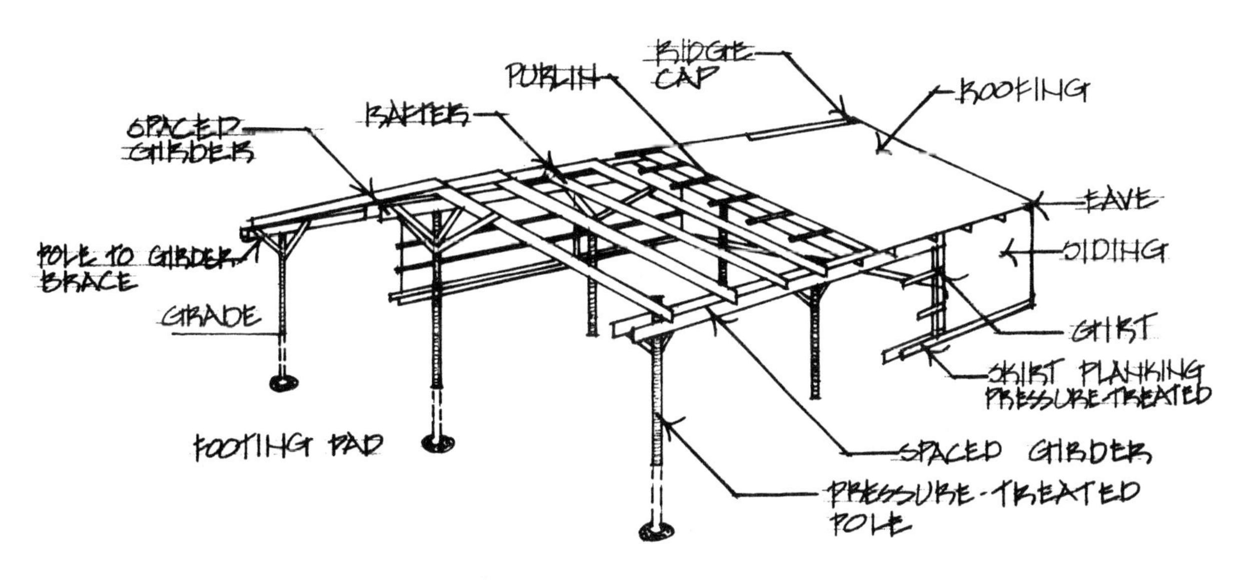


POLE FRAME CONSTRUCTION

# Siting Your Barn

Before you can start building your barn, or even apply for a building permit, you'll need to "site" your barn, which means placing it on your lot. Even if you have a large piece of land, the location of your barn may be determined more by zoning regulations, utility cost, and other factors beyond just where you'd like to put it.

This site planning checklist will help you determine how much flexibility you really do have, as well as help you assess what requirements the local authorities may have that affect where you place your barn.

***SITE PLANNING CHECKLIST***

1. What is the zoning on the property?
2. Are any zoning variances required to build a barn?
3. Does the local building code allow you to build a barn?
4. Are there any homeowner's association restrictions on your property?
5. Do you have space for other related uses around the barn site?
6. Are any easements necessary for roads and utilities to the barn?
7. How much will it cost to extend utilities, such as electricity and water, to the barn?
8. What type of soil is at the building site?
9. Is there good drainage at the building site?
10. How will your neighbors be affected by your barn?

***ZONING***

Most areas have zoning ordinances to regulate property use and development. Check with your local authorities to find out if your barn, and the proposed use for the barn, is permitted.

This is especially important if you plan a home-based business, even one as simple as raising a few animals. Many local zoning laws control not just the use, but the scope and size of the use. For example, you may be able to raise a hog, or two, for your own use, but commercial hog production would be prohibited.

Local zoning regulations also often regulate the size and height of buildings, so be sure to verify that your proposed barn meets the requirements. Many zoning codes use the "apparent" height of a building, rather than the actual height at the peak.

You can calculate the apparent height of a building by measuring the height at the eave, or lowest part of the roof, and then at the peak. Half the distance between the eave and the peak is the "apparent height". For example, if a barn's roof is 12 feet from the ground at the eaves, and 20 feet at the peak, the apparent height is 16 feet.

### *ZONING VARIANCES*

If your barn, or the proposed use of the barn, does not meet the zoning regulations, you may need to get a variance. If your proposed building, or its use, is reasonably close to the existing regulations, or their "intent", the odds are in your favor that you can get a variance to build.

In my experience, the most common variance granted is for height restrictions. Your community might have a 16 foot height restriction, but chances are quite good you'll be able to get a variance for a two story barn with an apparent height of 18 feet.

### *BUILDING CODES*

Like zoning ordinances, building codes can affect what you can build on your property. For example, building codes often specify the percentage of a lot that can be used for buildings and "hard surfaces", such as driveways. If your new barn exceeds the maximum area, you won't be able to get a permit. Your local building officials will be able to give you the specific requirements for your lot.

### *HOMEOWNER'S ASSOCIATIONS*

In most developments or subdivisions, restrictions on the use of the property—or the size and style of the buildings—affect what you can, or cannot, build on your lot. These restrictions, commonly called CC&Rs (covenants, conditions and restrictions) are legally binding, just like zoning restrictions. If your property is affected by CC&Rs, make sure you meet the requirements, or apply for a variance, before you apply for a building permit.

### *RELATED USES*

In addition to providing room for your barn, be sure to allow room for other barn-related facilities. For example, if you're building a horse barn, plan for corrals, exercise areas, bedding and manure storage, and parking and turn-around areas for horse trailers and hay delivery trucks.

### *UTILITY EASEMENTS*

You'll need to check with local utilities to make sure that they can bring utilities to your proposed barn site. Often the best, or least expensive, route to provide access and utilities is not the one you have an easement for. Paying a neighbor for a utility easement is sometimes cheaper than paying the power company for a longer route.

### WATER AND POWER

Talk to your local utility company before you start construction to make sure they can extend utilities to your building site at a reasonable cost. If your property is served by an on-site well, make sure it's not downhill from your new barn if you're planning on keeping animals. Most building codes require a 100-foot protective zone setback between a well and buildings, or septic systems, to prevent possible contamination of the drinking water from animal manure or sewage.

### SOIL TYPE

The soil type at your building site can affect the design of your barn foundation. Some soils will not hold much weight, and may require larger footings or a special foundation design. Other soils can trap moisture, causing wintertime frost heave if it's not deep enough. Be sure to talk to local building professionals, who are familiar with local soil conditions.

### GOOD DRAINAGE

The ideal building site would have well-drained soil and a slope of about 5 feet in 100 feet away from the building, in all directions, to provide surface drainage. Stay away from areas with obvious drainage problems, such as a spot at the base of a slope, where water runoff could create a problem, or wet areas caused by high groundwater.

It also goes without saying that you should never build in any areas that flood. Almost all counties have excellent flood-plain maps that show 100-year flood lines. Your county probably would not issue a building permit if you're in a 100-year flood plain, but it doesn't hurt to check it yourself.

### THE NEIGHBORS

While your new barn, and the animals who will live in it, may be a dream come true for you, your neighbors may have entirely different opinions. Here are a few tips on how to be a good neighbor:

- Keep your neighbors informed from the start of your building project. Try to work with them to handle any objections they may have to your barn and animals.
- Compost, or remove, manure frequently to control smells and insects.
- Install and maintain the proper fencing required to control your animals.
- The law considers many animals, such as horses, an "attractive nuisance".

You are liable for the actions of your animals, so make sure your neighbors' children understand that they are allowed on the property only when you invite them.

- Other nuisances that may upset your neighbors include excess noise, offensive odors and heavy traffic. Remember to practice the "Golden Rule" when dealing with your neighbors.

#### *BUILDING "ON THE SQUARE"*

Architect Donald Berg, in his book *Barns and Backbuildings,* points out a simple, but powerful rule of site planning. Traditional homesteads always built their outbuildings "on the square" with each other, with all walls at right angles or parallel to each other, no matter how far apart the buildings. This provides a visual character that he calls "a hallmark of American farm architecture".
So try to align your new barn "on the square" with any existing buildings on your property. That way it will look "just right."

# Estimating Costs

Contrary to popular belief, building contractors aren't necessarily experts, who know everything about construction. Most are simply well-organized project managers. They've learned to "work smarter, not harder". You don't need to know how to pour concrete, frame a wall, or hang a door to manage your own building project and save a bundle.

There are plenty of capable subcontractors out there who can do a great job for you. All you need to do is find them, schedule and coordinate their work, and pay them when the work is done.

**_You don't need to know how to pour concrete, frame a wall, or hang a door to manage your own building project and save a bundle!_**

Managing a barn-building project entails careful planning, organization and managing people. In the following chapters, you'll learn how to effectively estimate the cost of your building project, establish a budget, select and manage the subcontractors, and work with building inspectors to ensure that the building meets code requirements.

Even if you've never done it before, the information you'll learn in the next few chapters will give you the knowledge and confidence to successfully take your building project from an idea to reality—on time and on budget!

**_A fax machine is an essential tool to help you speed the flow of bids, quotes, change orders and other communications between you, as project manager, and the many others involved in the project. The small price of a basic fax will pay for itself in the first week of your building project._**

### Estimating costs

Preparing a cost estimate and setting a budget for your building project is the essential first step in the building process. Without a realistic idea of the cost, you haven't a clue whether or not you can afford to build your "dream" barn. If a bank or other lending institution is involved, they will usually require a written estimate before making a lending commitment.

At this point, you're probably wondering just where to begin. For a quick overview of costs, you can use the square foot costs found in the "National Building Costs Manual", available at your local library or from the publisher, Craftsman Book Company, (800) 829-8123, or online at www.craftsman-book.com. Craftsman also has several construction estimating books to help you produce a detailed and accurate cost estimate for your barn.

Most stock plans include a material list that typically covers the materials used for the "shell" of a building. You'll need to add costs for interior finish, such as stall components, plumbing, wiring and site improvements.

To help you produce an accurate and detailed estimate of construction costs, I've included two construction cost schedules for your use. You'll find full-size forms in Chapter 14 to copy and use on your own project.

**CONSTRUCTION COST SCHEDULE**

| EXPENSE | ESTIMATE | ACTUAL COST |
|---|---|---|
| Cabinets | | |
| Carpentry, Finish | | |
| Carpentry, Framing | | |
| Concrete Flatwork | | |
| Contingency Funds | | |
| Doors & Windows | | |
| Drywall | | |
| Electrical | | |
| Excavation | | |
| Fencing & Gates | | |
| Foundation | | |
| Gutters | | |
| Flooring | | |
| Heating System | | |
| Insurance | | |
| Landscaping | | |
| Loan Costs | | |
| Lumber, Finish | | |
| Lumber, Framing | | |
| Masonry | | |
| Paint/Stain | | |
| Paving | | |
| Permits | | |
| Plans | | |
| Plumbing | | |
| Roofing | | |
| Sand & Gravel | | |
| Siding & Trim | | |
| Stall Components | | |
| Utilities | | |
| Ventilation System | | |
| Misc. Labor | | |
| Misc. Materials | | |
| TOTAL COST | | |

This cost estimating schedule allows you to include all the costs of your project, including loan costs, fencing, etc. The "Contingency Funds" are a percentage allowance to cover things that you might forget, unforeseen extras that add to the overall expense, and the inevitable mistakes that crop up in the course of any building project. If this is your first time managing a building project, I'd recommend that you add a 10 percent contingency fund to your total estimate.

**BUILDING COST SCHEDULE**

| DESCRIPTION | USE | QUANTITY & SIZE |
|---|---|---|
| Concrete – Footings | Footings & Piers | |
| Concrete – Walls | Foundation Walls | |
| Concrete – Slab | Floor | |
| Reinforcing Steel | Foundation Re-bar | |
| Anchor Bolts | Wall Anchor Bolts | |
| Floor Joists or Trusses | Wood Floor Joists | |
| Floor Sheathing | Wood Floor Sheathing | |
| Support Beams | Wood or Steel Beams | |
| Support Posts | Beam Support Posts | |
| Wall Plates | Wall Top/Bottom Plates | |
| Wall Studs | Wall Framing | |
| Window/Door Headers | Header Beams | |
| Rafters & Cross-Ties | Roof Framing | |
| Manufactured Trusses | Alternate Roof Framing | |
| Roof Sheathing | Roof Sheathing | |
| Roof Underlayment | Underlayment | |
| Roofing | Roofing | |
| Roof Flashing & Vents | Roof Protection | |
| Wall Sheathing | Exterior Walls | |
| Siding | Exterior Walls | |
| Trim Lumber | Wall & Roof Trim | |
| Framing Hardware | [illegible] | |
| Windows | Exterior Windows | |
| Doors | Exterior Doors | |
| Nails | Framing & Finish | |
| Interior Framing | Interior Partitions/Stalls | |
| | | |
| | | |
| | | |
| | | |
| | | |
| | | |
| | | |
| | | |

The next cost estimating schedule, the Building Cost Schedule, looks at just the materials that go into the barn, such as lumber and roofing. When this is completed, you'll have an accurate material list to give to lumberyards for bids. To help you prepare a material list, here are some pointers on each line item in the schedule.

## Concrete

It's easier to calculate how much concrete you'll need if you use a few simple formulas. Concrete is sold by the cubic yard, which contains 27 cubic feet. Formula One: Length x width x depth divided by 27 = cubic yards. For example, most foundation footings are 8" deep by 16" wide, so your footings will require .88 cubic feet of concrete per lineal foot of footing. Since pouring footings is a sloppy job at best, figure 1 cubic foot of concrete per lineal foot of footing.

Foundation walls are calculated the same way, length x width x depth. A typical foundation wall that was 8" wide by 24" deep would require 1.34 cubic feet of concrete (.67 x 2 =1.34) per lineal foot of wall.

### CONCRETE SLABS

Concrete slabs, which are usually 4 inches thick , require 1 cubic yard of concrete per 81 square feet of floor area. A 1200 square-foot concrete slab, for example, would require a shy 15 cubic yards. If you're pouring a thicker concrete slab, recalculate the quantity as follows: The same 1200 square-foot concrete slab in a 5 inch thickness would require 1 cubic yard of concrete per 65 square feet, or 19 yards, and a 6-inch thick slab would require 1 cubic yard per 54 square feet, or a total of 22 yards.

| Slab thickness | Coverage per cubic yard |
|---|---|
| 4 inches | 81 square feet |
| 5 inches | 65 square feet |
| 6 inches | 54 square feet |

### REINFORCING STEEL

Reinforcing steel for most small buildings is 1/2-inch in diameter. Most codes call for two horizontal pieces spaced evenly in the footing, and one piece every 18 inches both horizontally and vertically in the foundation wall. To calculate for a typical 20 x 24 barn foundation, with 98 lineal feet of foundation, you would multiply 4 x 98 (two in footing, two in walls) or 392 lineal feet, plus one two-foot vertical "stick" of rebar every eighteen inches, for a total of 65 "sticks" or 130 lineal feet. Most lumberyards sell rebar precut to 24" lengths specifically for foundations. Add 10 percent for splices and piers.

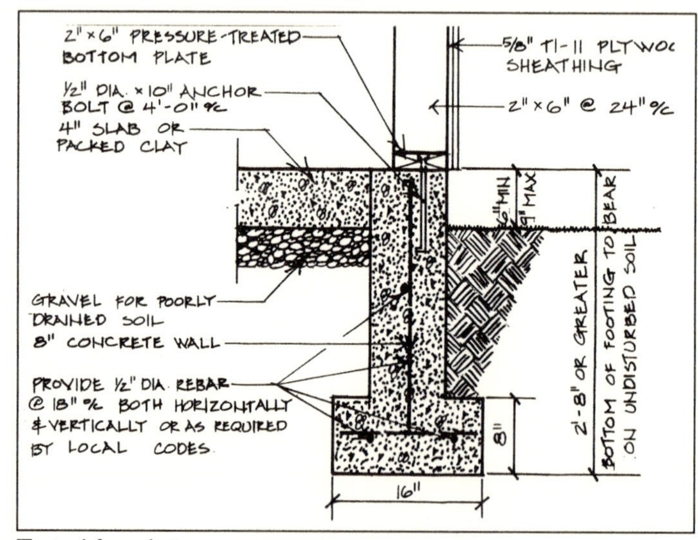

Typical foundation cross-section

### *ANCHOR BOLTS*

Anchor bolts are commonly ½-inch x 10 inches and spaced 48 inches apart. The pressure-treated sill plate is bolted to the foundation with these anchor bolts. To estimate the total number you'll need, divide the total length of foundation walls by four, then add one bolt for each corner and two for each door opening. Stricter building codes call for 2-inch-square "bearing plates," instead of washers, to better distribute the load at each anchor bolt. Check to see what your local code requires.

### *PRESSURE-TREATED SILLS*

The sills—also called plates—are pressure-treated with a preservative to prevent rot and insect damage, and can be used as the only bottom plate or under an untreated bottom plate. Most good builders add a strip of "sill-sealer", a closed-cell foam strip that keeps out bugs and drafts, under the treated sill just before it's bolted to the foundation wall. Add up the total perimeter length of your foundation walls to determine how many lineal feet of sill are required.

### *FLOOR JOISTS*

Floor joists are used to support the main floor of a building where a concrete slab is not used, as well as the loft floor. The plans will often include a floor framing plan, to make estimating much easier. If not, the size and spacing of the floor joists will be noted elsewhere on the plans.

Using the typical 20 x 24 barn with joists on 2 foot centers, you'll need thirteen 20' joists, plus 48 lineal feet of rim joist (also called band joist) for the two long sides. With a joist spacing of 16" on center, you'll need nineteen 20' joists, plus rim joists.

### *FLOOR TRUSSES*

Floor trusses are slowly replacing traditional sawn-wood joists, as larger logs become more expensive. As I write this, manufactured wood joists, which look like miniature I-beams are about 20-30 percent less expensive than sawn lumber, such as 2 x 10s, in most areas.

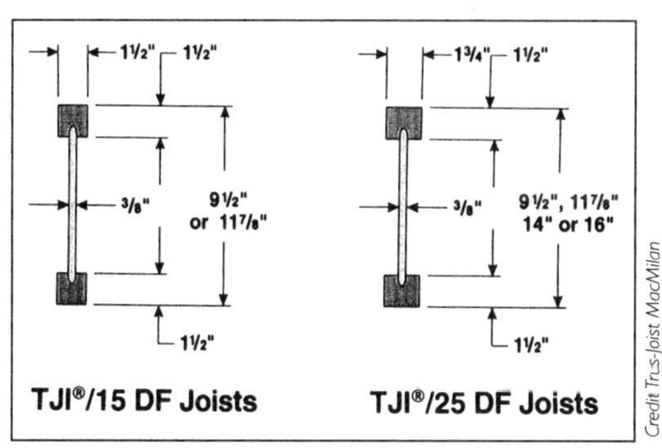

Trus-joist

Carpenters also appreciate the fact that they are lighter, and easier to install, with no "crown" to worry about. Often you can substitute I-beam wood joists for traditional joists and clear span an entire barn, eliminating one or more beams and the support posts.

Check with your local lumberyard for the latest on the types of manufactured I-beams available in your area. Most manufacturers publish span tables that allow you to easily calculate the floor joist size and spacing, based on the loads you plan to place on the floor system. This allows you to tailor the system to your needs, whether it's hay to the ceiling or lighter uses.

#### *FLOOR SHEATHING*

Floor sheathing is nailed or screwed to the floor joists in a wood floor system. It can be a finish floor, or a sub-floor for a finish floor, such as tile or carpet. Most builders use ¾-inch exterior grade plywood or OSB (oriented strand board). For our typical 20 x 24 barn, divide the square footage (480) by 32 (the square footage in a 4' x 8' plywood sheet) to get the number of sheets needed (15). Most good builders also glue the floor sheathing to the joists, as it can add up to 20 percent more strength and stiffness to the floor system.

#### *SUPPORT BEAMS AND POSTS*

Support beams and posts are used to support the floor joists at mid-span, or to provide support for a second floor, such as in a monitor-style barn. Often when joists span 20 feet or less, the beams and posts can be eliminated by using manufactured floor trusses. Most plans will specify the species (such as fir or pine), grade and size of any support beams and posts, so it's simply a matter of entering the correct lengths on your estimate form.

As with trusses, there are many composite materials available today that are lighter, stronger and often cheaper than full-size sawn-timber beams. Check with your local lumberyard to see what beam substitutes are available, such as Glue-lam™, Micro-lam™ and Versa-lam™ beams.

#### *WALL PLATES*

Wall plates are the horizontal framing at the top and bottom of each wall. With one plate at the bottom and a double plate at the top, just multiply the total length of all walls by three to get the total footage needed. Most framers prefer to order the longest lengths available (16' to 20' are typical) for stronger framing. Add 10 percent for scrap.

#### *WALL STUDS*

Wall studs are the vertical wall framing, spaced on either 16-inch or 24-inch centers. You can buy precut studs in standard lengths, but the quality of the lumber is better if you order "standard and better" (#2 grade) in the lengths you want, typically 8' to 10', and trim it to the exact length you need. As a general "rule of thumb", you can figure one stud for every lineal foot of wall, plus two studs for each corner. Don't subtract for door and window openings—this allows extra material for blocking and bracing.

### HEADERS

Headers are the beams placed over all openings, such as windows and doors, in load-bearing walls. The plans will often specify header sizes. Here is another area where "composite beams" are being used more and more, such as Versa-lams™ and Glue-lams™. Check with your local lumberyard to see what's available in your area. For your estimate, add the width of each opening, plus 1 foot each.

### RAFTERS

Rafters are best estimated by doing a count from the roof framing plan, which will give you both the quantity needed and lengths. Be sure to round up to the next 2-foot multiple to allow for the plumb cut on each end. If there is no roof framing plan, you can measure the rafter lengths from the cross-section plan.

Rafters are typically placed on 2-foot centers, so divide the length of the building by 2, and add one extra rafter pair for the end, to get the quantity you'll need. Manufactured trusses are also spaced on 2-foot centers, but the manufacturer usually will quote the roof system as a package. Most roof truss manufacturers will require a set of construction plans to give you a bid, which includes setting the trusses on top of the walls. If you want the boom truck to also help tilt up the trusses, it's usually rented by the hour.

### ROOF SHEATHING

Roof sheathing is most often plywood or OSB (oriented strand board) and comes in standard 4 x 8 foot sheets. To estimate the number of sheets you'll need to cover the roof, multiply the length of a rafter by the length of the roof, including overhangs. This number will give you the area of one side of the roof. Next, double the number to get the total square footage for both sides of the roof. Now, divide the total square footage by 32, which is the number of square feet in a sheet of plywood. This is how many sheets of plywood or OSB you'll need. Add 10 percent to the total to allow for waste.

### ROOFING

Roofing is sold by the "square", which is 100 square feet. Most asphalt composition shingles come three bundles to the square, while cedar shingles and shakes are four bundles per square. When estimating the amount of roofing required, don't forget the overhangs at the eaves and gable ends. To allow for scrap and the starter course of roofing at the eaves, add 1.5 square feet to the total for each lineal foot of valleys, hips, ridge and eaves.

### *ROOFING FELT*

Roofing felt, or underlayment, is rolled out on the roof sheathing before the roofing is applied. The standard 15# felt comes in 300-square-foot rolls. Add 20 percent to the total roof area to allow for overlap and waste.

### *ROOF FLASHING*

Roof flashing is used around skylights, chimneys, dormers and valleys. The roofing subcontractor can tell you what is customarily used in your area, and the quantity to order.

### *VENTING*

Venting is usually done with a combination of eave and ridge vents. "Bird blocks", small screened vents in a 2 x 4 or 2 x 6 nailed between the rafters or trusses, are the most common method of eave venting. Bird blocks can be purchased at most lumberyards or ordered with a truss package. At the ridge, a continuous ridge vent, made of plastic and installed under the ridge shingles, is widely used, as are "clamshell" roof vents.

The traditional cupola will also provide good ventilation, and is a perfect decorative "cap" for a traditional style barn. The cupola plans in this book are adaptable to any size barn, and are designed to be "owner-builder" friendly, with simplified construction techniques.

### *WALL SHEATHING*

Wall sheathing is estimated by adding up the total length of all exterior walls, then multiplying by the wall height. Do not subtract for window and door openings. To calculate any gable ends, multiply the width by the center height, and divide by two. Add 10 percent to the total to cover waste.

### *SIDING*

Siding is estimated just like wall sheathing. If you're using plywood or other panel siding, find the total square footage and add 10 percent for waste. If you're using another type of siding, you'll need to check with your local lumberyard to determine how much to add to your square footage. Bevel siding, for example, requires 33 percent more material than the actual square footage covered.

### *TRIM LUMBER*

Specifications, such as the size of eave and gable-end trim boards, are usually included in the plans. Simply total the lineal feet of eave and gable-end trim shown on the plans, and add 10 percent for waste. The size of corner, window, and door trim is determined by the look you are trying to achieve. 4-inch wide trim is a common size.

### FRAMING HARDWARE

Framing hardware is an essential part of most building projects. Anchor bolts hold the foundation to the walls. Hurricane ties can keep a roof from flying away in a storm. These metal connectors, and others, are noted in most plans, but you need to calculate the quantities. Hurricane ties, for example, are used wherever a truss or rafter meets a wall, so multiplying the number of trusses or rafters times two will give you the quantity needed. Be sure to check the detail drawings to catch any specialized connectors, such as post-to-beam connectors that may need to be special ordered.

### WINDOWS

Windows are specified in the floor plan by the size and type of window, such as a 5'0" x 3'6" slider. The first number is the width, in feet and inches, the second is the height. In general, vinyl windows are the best choice for most building projects, as they are affordable, low maintenance, energy efficient, and can be ordered in almost any size and style you might want.

### DOORS

Door sizes are also specified in the floor plan, but you'll need to determine what style and swing will work best for you. To keep costs down, many builders fabricate their own doors, either from "scratch", or with a frame kit from Country Manufacturing (www.countrymfg.com).

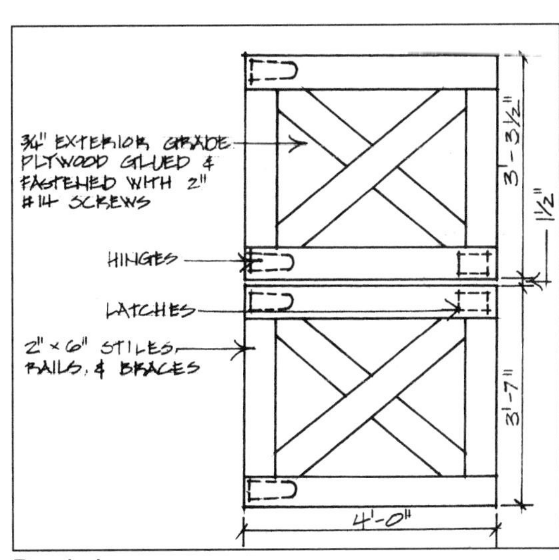

Dutch door

Larger sliding doors, such as the main door to a center aisle barn, can be site-built using stock track and roller hardware, made by National Manufacturing, readily available through lumberyards and home centers.

### INTERIOR FRAMING

Interior framing is estimated much the same way as exterior walls. Most owner-builders will find that buying stall components from one of the resources listed in Chapter 14 is a cost-effective approach. Using the prefabricated metal parts, plus locally available lumber, allows you to quickly build safe and sturdy stalls for your animals.

# Project Scheduling

### *FULL CONSTRUCTION SCHEDULE*

The **Construction Schedule** shows the sequence of steps in building a barn, listed in the approximate order they take place. Subcontractors and suppliers are busy people, so don't expect them to jump when you call, and arrive on the job a day or two later. That's where the first column, "schedule" comes in.

Before you start scheduling your subcontractors, find out how much advance notice they will need, and how much time to complete the job. Once you have that information, you can start filling in the schedule.

**CONSTRUCTION SCHEDULE**

| EXPENSE | Schedule | Start | Finish |
|---|---|---|---|
| Temporary power | | | |
| Building permits | | | |
| Utility easements | | | |
| Clearing/Excavation | | | |
| Foundation | | | |
| Buried plumbing | | | |
| Concrete slab | | | |
| Backfill foundation | | | |
| Shell framing | | | |
| Rough-in plumbing | | | |
| Rough-in electrical | | | |
| Masonry | | | |
| Roofing | | | |
| Gutters | | | |
| Exterior doors | | | |
| Exterior windows | | | |
| Siding/Trim | | | |
| Exterior paint/Stain | | | |
| Final grading | | | |
| Insulation | | | |
| Interior walls/Stalls | | | |
| Interior floors | | | |
| Plumbing fixtures | | | |
| Electrical fixtures | | | |
| Move-In! | | | |

Here's how: In the "Schedule" column, write the date when you need to call and schedule a contractor, based on how much advance notice they say they need. In the "Start" column, note the date you want the contractor on the job. In the "Finish" column, note the date when the contractor should be finished.

| | Schedule | Start | Finish |
|---|---|---|---|
| Temporary power | | | |
| Building permits | | | |
| Utility easements | | | |
| Clearing/Excavation | March 28 | April 18 | April 19 |
| Foundation | March 13 | April 20 | April 25 |
| Buried plumbing | | | |
| Concrete slab | | | |
| Backfill foundation | | | |
| Shell framing | | | |

Here's an example of how the scheduling process works. You call the excavating contractor and find he needs three weeks advance notice, and it will take him two days to finish the job. Let's say you want him to start on April 18, which you note in the "Start" column. Next, note April 19 in the "Finish" column. Then in the "Schedule" column, note March 28, the date you need to call and schedule him.

Your foundation contractor wants five weeks notice, and five days to form up and pour the foundation. You know the excavating contractor should be done on April 19, so you schedule the foundation contractor for April 20 in the "Start" column. In the "Finish" column, note April 25, the day he expects to complete the foundation. In the "Schedule" column, note March 13, the date you need to call him to schedule the foundation work.

The construction schedule will save you (and your contractors and subcontractors) time, money and frustration. It's best to use a pencil to fill out the schedule, as it's easier to make any changes that may be necessary. You should also not try to schedule too tightly, so if a contractor is late or runs over schedule, the rest of the schedule does not need to be changed.

Try not to schedule two contractors at the same time, even if it affects your schedule a bit. Most subs prefer to have the job site to themselves so they don't have to compete for limited temporary power or get in each other's way, and have ample space to spread out their materials and tools.

> ***"Eighty percent of success is just showing up."***
> ***— Woody Allen***

In addition to using the Construction Schedule for contractors, make sure that any supplies required for each phase of construction can be on the building site when needed. For example, windows and doors may require several weeks between the order date and the delivery date.

When your local building department issues a building permit, you'll receive a list of the required inspections. Note these on the schedule next to the phase of construction, using an "I" or highlighting the work that needs to be inspected. For example, any rough-in plumbing that will be covered after a concrete slab is poured needs to be inspected before the pour takes place. The most common inspections required for a barn are:

- Footing and setback inspection—before concrete is poured.
- Foundation walls—before concrete is poured.
- Under-slab plumbing—before concrete is poured.
- Framing and rough-in plumbing—after roof is on.
- Rough-in electrical—after roof is on.
- Final inspection—after the building is complete.

# Codes and Regulations

In August of 1992, Hurricane Andrew's 160-m.p.h. winds destroyed more than 80,000 South Florida homes in just four hours. In the months and years following this disaster, a small army of engineers, inspectors and insurance investigators put together the true story of what really caused such widespread destruction of buildings.

It wasn't faulty building codes. They were considered tough even before Hurricane Andrew. If they had been followed, much of the destruction would have been prevented. Inspectors found roof sheathing panels attached with just four nails, missing hurricane clips that could have kept walls and roof together, and incorrectly installed roof bracing. The real villains, in many instances were sloppy builders and subcontractors, whose work was passed by overworked or indifferent building inspectors.

Major disasters, such as fires, earthquakes, tornados and hurricanes, like Andrew, are why building codes were developed. Most building codes focus on structural, fire safety and life safety areas, as they should. Codes are not static regulations, but constantly changing in response to new materials, changing lifestyles, and learning from experience. For example, after several residential decks collapsed, building code officials adopted tougher standards for connecting decks to houses to prevent future tragedies.

Most building codes are a sensible way to protect lives, prevent problems, and keep buildings from falling down. Strange as it may seem, there is currently no single national building code, although the new "International Residential Code" is being adopted in more areas.

There are currently three building codes used in the United States; the *Uniform Building Code* in the Western states, the *Standard Building Code* in the Southern states, and the *National Building Code* in the Midwest and Northeast. Most cities, towns and counties use these codes as a basis for their local codes, modified to suit local conditions. Your local library should have a copy of the current codebook in the reference section. Your local building department will often have several one-or-two-page handouts that cover important sections of the code, such as the requirements for a code-approved safe stairway.

One book that has been extremely helpful to other owner-builders is *Code-Check: A Field Guide to Building a Safe House,* a condensed guide to the most commonly found code violations found by building inspectors. The author, a building inspector frustrated by seeing the same code violations over and over again, put the guide together to help people avoid repeating the same mistakes. Check out the book at your local library, bookstore or at the author's web site, www.codecheck.com

To help you build a barn that complies with the building codes, let's review a few of the basic requirements, applicable in almost all parts of the United States. This is not intended to be a complete list, but rather a sampling of the most common and sensible codes that apply to barns.

### *EXCAVATION*

The very first step in the actual building process is excavating for the foundation, whether it's a poured-concrete foundation or simply treated poles buried in the ground. The code requires that the foundation be placed on solid ground, not loose fill or buried stumps. If you find anything but "undisturbed" soil, you'll need to keep going until you reach some. Otherwise, you run the risk of the foundation settling or cracking, as the unstable soil underneath it settles over time.

### *FROST LINE*

If you're building in Hawaii, skip this section! Otherwise, check with your local building department to determine the depth of your local "frost line". When the ground freezes, any moisture it contains causes it to expand, causing "frost heave". If your foundation doesn't extend below the frost line, this frost heave can cause serious damage. This is why all building codes require that a foundation extend below the local frost line.

If you live in an area where the frost line is deep enough to make foundations expensive, you might want to investigate the "Frost-Protected Shallow Foundation "FPSF" used in more than one million Scandinavian homes. Frank Lloyd Wright used the FPSF in his "Usonian" homes. To learn more, you can read a free online report at www.huduser.org. Click on "search", then type in the keyword FPSF.

### *FOOTINGS*

The footing is the base of a foundation that rests on the solid ground mentioned earlier. Most codes call for a minimum 6-inch-deep by 12-inch-wide footing for a single story building, and an 8-inch-deep by 16-inch-wide footing for a two story building. Most codes also require two horizontal pieces of ½-inch rebar in the footings to reinforce the concrete.

### *FOUNDATION WALLS*

Most building codes permit both block walls and poured-concrete walls for foundations. The code will also specify the strength of the concrete, typically 2500 pounds per square inch, but for most foundations, a "five sack" mix (trade talk for five-ninety pound sacks of cement per cubic yard) is used to provide the required strength. Codes are being revised to provide for more reinforcing steel in foundation walls to provide extra strength under stresses, such as earthquakes. In our area, for example, the codes have gone from no rebar required at all, to 18" on center, both vertical and horizontal. Your local building department can give you their requirements.

### *PRESSURE-TREATED LUMBER*

Building codes require the use of pressure-treated wood where it comes in contact with the ground, or concrete, or masonry, as well as for termite protection. Treated wood that is code-approved for ground contact, such as the structural posts used in a pole-frame barn, must be stamped "ground contact .60". The number, .60, is the amount of preservative in the lumber, in pounds per cubic foot. Building codes typically allow a .40 pcf concentration for non-structural lumber.

The Environmental Protection Agency has determined there a risk of contamination to drinking water due to the current treatment process. It uses arsenic, and it will be phased out by 2004. A new process, still using copper as the primary preservative, will replace the current process, and should be much safer. Ask your local lumberyard if they have the new arsenic-free treated lumber. For more information, see www.preservedwood.com.

### *STRUCTURAL FRAMING*

Because the framing of a wood-frame building is such an important part of its structural integrity, the building codes devote a lot of space to the acceptable standards. Review your local codes to see what's required in the following areas:

- **Nailing Schedule**—Specifies the number, spacing and size of nails for each framing connection. For example, the code requirement for nailing wall sheathing is 6d (2-inch) nails spaced 6 inches on center on panel edges and 12 inches on center at intermediate supports.

- **Columns and Posts**—The code requires any columns or posts, exposed to the weather or water splash, be preservative-treated lumber or raised off the floor with a metal, or concrete, pedestal.

- **Headers** —The beams that support window, door and other openings must be adequate to carry the loads imposed. The building code will specify values for various species and grades of wood that can be used to calculate safe spans for each size of beam. Most building departments now use "Beam-Check" software to calculate safe header sizes in the plan review process. The manufacturers of Glulam™ (glued and laminated) beams publish easy to use tables that allow you to calculate the correct size glulam header for a given load and span.

- **Floor Joists** —Are required by the code to hold a given load without excessive "deflection", or bounce. Most codes will specify the size, species, and grade of lumber to be used for a given span to meet the requirements. The code allows joists to be spaced 16" on center, or 24" on center, as long as they meet the strength and stiffness test.

***The Western Wood Products Association has a span calculator used for beams, headers, floor joists, and rafters. Go to www.wwpa.org and click on "publications," then go to "span calculator."***

- **I-Joists** —With the growing scarcity of larger dimension lumber, such as 2 x 10s and 2 x 12s often used for joists, manufactured I-joists are becoming an affordable and more commonly used alternative. Your local lumberyard can give you more information on the brands they carry, as well as span tables.

- **Rafters** —Are required by the codes to do much the same as floor joists, plus handle snow loads. Your local building code should provide span tables to help you choose the correct size rafter. If you plan to insulate the rafter cavity, you'll need to make sure there is room for the insulation you need, plus one inch, or more, above the insulation for ventilation. Manufactured I-joists may be an economical choice for rafters, too.

- **Wall Framing** —Codes specify the size, grade and spacing for wall and partition framing. Most codes require studs at 16" centers, when using *stud* (#3) grade, and 24" centers, when using *standard and better* (#2) grade lumber. Keep in mind that a wall framed with 2"x 6" studs, on 24" centers, uses the same amount of lumber (total board footage) as a wall framed with 2" x 4" studs, on 16" centers. Since it is possible to pack 50 percent more insulation in a six inch wall, it's the best choice for a heated building, considering the lumber cost is the same.

- **Bracing**—In order to provide structural resistance to forces like wind loads and earthquakes, codes specify bracing for floors, walls and roofs. Correctly installed, plywood or OSB board provides adequate bracing. With most smaller structures, simply sheathing the exterior walls with 1/2" plywood or OSB board is sufficient to provide bracing. If you are in a high-risk area, such as a hurricane, tornado or earthquake zone, pay particular attention to the bracing requirements of your local code.

- **Graded Lumber**—I've talked to many owner-builders who want to use a few trees from their own property for a building project. There's a mobile sawmill in almost every rural community, and the cost is much lower than "store bought" lumber. A word of warning before you start sawing. Check with your local building department to see if they permit the use of ungraded or rough-sawn lumber. Many do, but some building departments insist that an independent lumber grader approve the framing lumber before it can be used for structural purposes.

- **Metal Connectors**—As more and more is learned from firsthand experience about the effects of a hurricane or earthquake on a building, manufacturers have developed many new products to resist these forces of nature. The major building codes have adopted requirements in high-risk areas to provide a "continuous load path" of connectors from the foundation to the roof. Your local building department should have information on local requirements. A useful Web site is www.strongtie.com.

- **Stairs**—Since so many people are injured falling down stairs, building codes cover this area in great detail. Code requirements for "rise" (the vertical distance between each stair tread) and "run" (the width of each stair tread) typically call for an 8-inch maximum rise and a minimum run of 9 inches. A widely-used "rule of thumb" calls for the riser height plus the tread width to equal 17½" inches.

To access a loft that is not a living space, codes often permit a steeper stair, called a "ship's ladder". A prefab pull-down version is sold at most lumberyards and home centers.

The *Stair Builder's Handbook* is an essential tool for any stair builder. You can find it at your local library or from Craftsman Book Company, www.craftsman-book.com, or (800) 829-8123.

# Working with Building Inspectors

Building inspectors, like traffic cops and I.R.S. auditors, are public employees most of us only deal with only because we have no choice. Just remember: Theirs is the only game in town if you want to get a building permit. While the idea of protecting the public safety, with common sense building codes, is one that few will quarrel with, the uneven and inconsistent enforcement of codes has always been a challenge to anyone who builds.

In our rural community, the small staff of our local building department is consistently helpful and patient with owner-builders. They are able to review and approve most residential building projects within two or three weeks. A few miles away—and a world apart—a large and fast growing county has a small army of people employed by a bloated bureaucracy. Inaccurately named the "Building Services Department", it routinely takes more than a year to issue a building permit. It's gotten so bad that builders often hire consultants to move their permit applications through the permitting process.

Hopefully, you are planning to build in an area where the inspectors have the patience of Mother Teresa and the personality of Mister Rogers. I've always approached building inspectors, plan checkers, and others in the permit center with the attitude that they were part of my "building team" and would rather help me more than harm me, if given half a chance.

> ***"Arguing with a building inspector is like trying to saddle a cow. You work like hell, but what's the point?"***
> ***— A Montana builder***

Guess what? That approach usually works, probably because building inspectors appreciate being treated like normal human beings, too! Their only job is to protect you and your building project from unsafe building practices.

Let the inspectors know that you appreciate their help, because you, too, want to build a safe and sound building you can be proud of. If there is a portion of the building codes you don't understand, ask for an explanation in a polite manner.

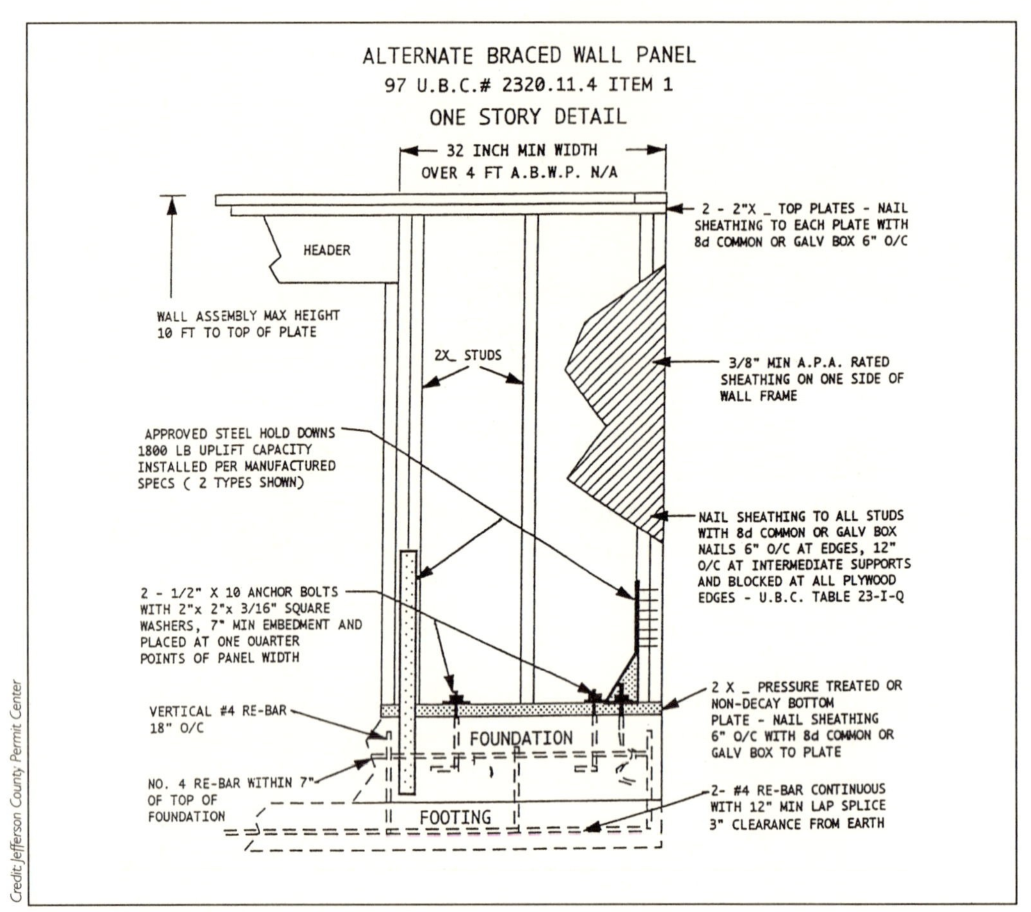


Credit: Jefferson County Permit Center

Braced wall panel

Your first encounter with your local building department will likely be at the permit center. There you'll find the permit application forms and other building-code-related handouts. Our local permit center has, for example, a shear wall handout for garages. In an earthquake-prone area, the code requires additional bracing to provide "shear" resistance to earthquake movement.

If you had less than four feet, the situation with most garages, the solution was to bring in a structural engineer, who would do the calculations and engineer the panels to meet code for a few hundred dollars. But, as the permit clerk explained, all I really had to do is attach the shear wall handout to the plans turned in for a permit, and it would be accepted as a "prescriptive" approach, saving a bundle in engineering fees. So, you see, it pays to be pleasant to the staff at the permit center.

As a part of the permitting process, you'll need to furnish a "site plan" showing setbacks, existing structures on the property, etc. Often your city or county assessor's office or a local title company can provide a drawing of your property to use as a starting point for the site plan.

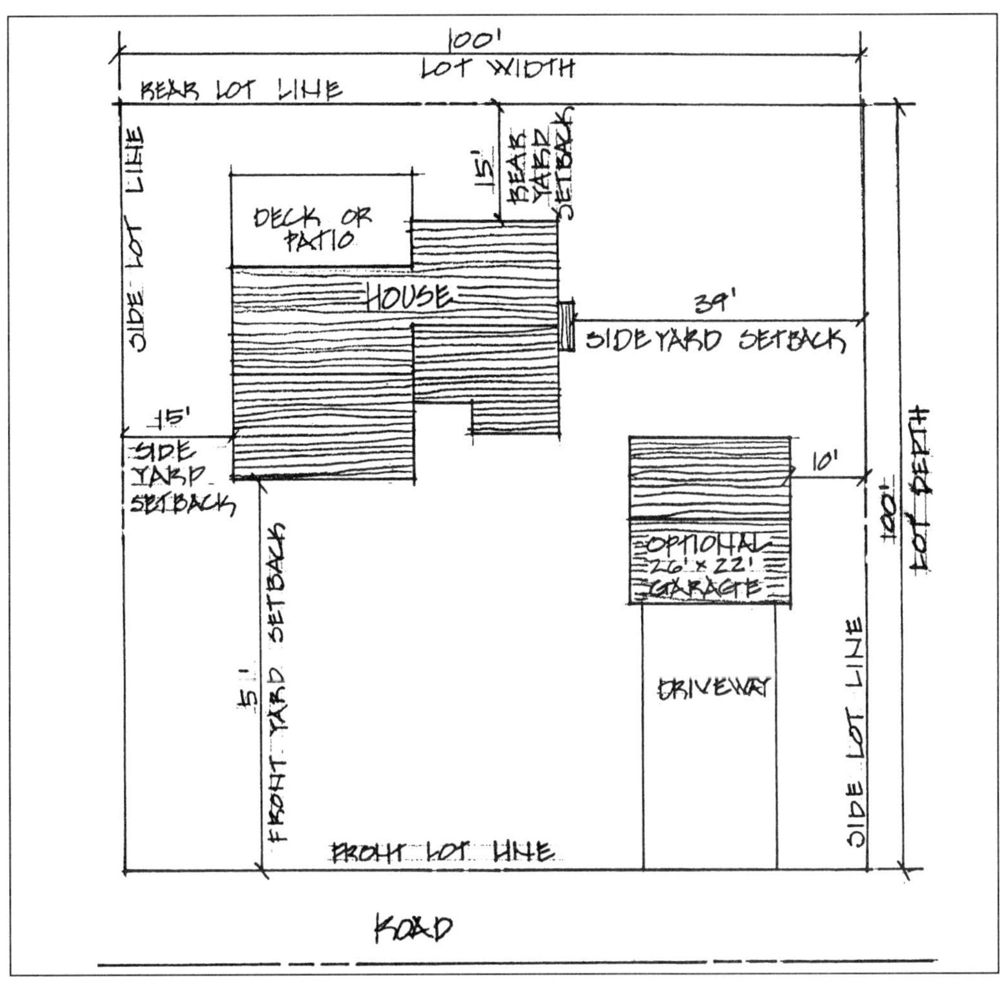


Sample site plan

At the time you pick up the permit application, you should be able to find out how long it will take for your permit to be issued, how much it will cost, and what inspections will be required.

Once you've turned in the permit application and plans, the application will be reviewed to make sure it complies with local regulations, and the plans checked for building code compliance. If there is any missing information on either, you'll get a phone call requesting more information.

It varies widely, but often code requirements, not indicated on the plans when you submit them, will be noted by the plan checker on the appropriate page in red ink. It might be as simple as noting the code required height of a stair handrail, or as complex as calling out shear wall requirements for exterior walls.

When the permit is issued, it will be subject to the added requirements noted on the plans. If there is anything you don't understand when your approved plans are returned, don't hesitate to ask. You don't want to redo work after it failed a field inspection!

When you're ready to start building, permit in hand, there will be a series of inspections at various stages in the construction process. These are the most common inspections for a simple building, such as a barn.

1. Footings and setbacks
2. Foundation
3. Under-slab plumbing
4. Framing and rough-in plumbing and electrical
5. Insulation (if applicable)
6. Sheetrock nailing (if applicable)
7. Final inspection

It's always a good idea to be on the building site when the inspector does the inspection. They can't give you an exact time, but will usually specify morning or afternoon. If the inspector is not going to pass something, you can find out why if you're on site during the inspection. In our small community, the field inspector will often sign off on the inspection if you promise to correct the error.

# Working with Subcontractors

Selecting the subcontractors for your building project can seem like an overwhelming challenge if you've never done it before. Good subcontractors can make the whole building process easy, exciting and fun. Bad subcontractors can make you wish you'd never started the project.

In this chapter, you'll learn a simple three-step process to find and evaluate subcontractors—how to pick the best and avoid the worst. You'll learn how to get bids that save you money, yet protect you from "low-ball" bids.

Most subcontractors take pride in their work, and appreciate a good working environment when they get to the building site. You'll learn how to ensure that you and your subs get along while working together. And finally, with a few simple precautions, you'll learn how to protect yourself from the unexpected situations that can arise in any building project.

## Finding good subs

You might think all you need to do is open the yellow pages, and call the subcontractors for bids. Sometimes you can find good contractors this way. However, I've found that contractors who advertise in the yellow pages tend to bid higher on most jobs than those who aren't listed.

Here's why. Many good subcontractors, whether they're framers or concrete finishers, don't like to advertise in the yellow pages because they have to waste too much time on what they call "price shoppers". The contractor will spend his unpaid time preparing a bid, only to find out the customer got six other bids—or already had another contractor picked—and was just hoping to find a better price.

Good subs are as busy as they want to be working for general contractors. Any new customers are typically a referral from an existing builder or owner-builder.

You'll want to find three subs for each trade you plan to use on your project. There are four simple ways to find the subs that are so good they don't need to advertise.

First, ask the suppliers. The local lumberyard knows the good framing subs. They probably can recommend a foundation and a roofing sub, too. The local ready-mix company delivers concrete to every building project with a foundation, and can be a good source for foundation and flatwork (concrete slabs) contractors.

Next, look around your area for current building projects, whether it's a single barn, garage, home, or an entire subdivision of homes. Often you'll get the names of several subs in a large development with several homes under construction.

> ***"Obstacles are those frightful things you see when you take your eyes off your goal."***
> ***— Henry Ford***

Don't hesitate to wander around and ask questions. If you see a well-done framing job, or a flawless concrete slab, ask who did it. If that sub isn't at the job site, chances are good someone else—often the general contractor or superintendent on site—can give you a name and phone number for the sub.

In rural areas, many building projects are tucked away in the woods, out of sight from a public road. Go to your local building department and ask for a list of recently-issued building permits. It's a public record, often published in the local paper. From this list, you'll probably find several barns or garages, together with the address of the building site and the owner's name.

Armed with your list, you can visit these "hidden" building sites, talk to contractors who are working on the projects, and look at their work. The owners are usually happy to let you know what they think about the contractor's work and tell you about their project, as well.

Many subcontractors, such as framing contractors, plumbers and electricians, belong to the local home builders association because that's where they get most of their work. Call your local HBA and ask for a copy of their membership list. Most give out the list at no charge, or will allow you to review it in their office.

Even if you don't find the specific sub you're looking for, you can always call one of the listed home builders and explain you're looking for a framing sub for your new barn. In most cases, builders are quite helpful, and willing to share the names of their subs with you.

Last, but not least, my own favorite way to find good subcontractors: Ask other subs. For example, if you've found a capable framer, ask who he recommends for a foundation sub. Since a foundation that's not perfectly level and square means extra work for the framers, you can be sure he'll recommend a sub whose work is excellent.

The foundation sub will likely know an excavator, who uses the latest laser-leveling technology to dig a foundation excavation that's within an inch or two of being perfectly flat, saving time and money for the foundation sub and you. You can see why it's in their best interest to give you the names of only the better subs.

## Obtaining bids

Now that you have a list of three specialty contractors for each phase of your building project, it's time for step two, getting bids from each of them. You may wonder why you need to get three bids for each phase of your building project. Trust me, after reviewing the bids, you'll see the reason for getting three. There can be quite a range of prices for the same work.

On a recent project, the difference in the foundation bids was 36 percent from low bidder to high. The framing bids differed by 22 percent from low to high; and the roofers had the largest spread, with the high bidder 45 percent higher than the low bidder.

Without multiple bids, you'll never know whether you're paying a high price or a fair price. In the above instance, the savings to the owner-builder from getting bids from three qualified subcontractors, for each phase, amounted to $3,489. What would you do with that kind of savings?

You might think, with such a range of prices, there would be something suspicious about the low bidder. Not necessarily. For example, my favorite electrician works alone, has one truck, does his own billing, and consistently underbids the larger electrical contractors, that have higher overhead, by 20 percent.

Another factor is the work load. When contractors are busy, they tend to bid new work higher than when things are slow. So, if you're getting bids from one extremely busy sub, and another, who's seeking more work, you'll probably see a similar wide range of bid prices.

Another benefit of getting multiple bids: Each sub will teach you something about his specialty that you might never have learned on your own. He might show you how to save money by changing an installation method, or substituting different materials. Here is a list of questions to ask when you're talking to contractors about bidding.

1. Do you usually supply materials? If so, ask for a bid with the materials and labor listed separately, so you can get a materials bid for cost comparison. Because of the overhead and bookkeeping involved, most materials get marked up at least 15 percent to cover those costs.
2. What information do you need to give me a bid?
3. What can we do to save money?
4. What are your scheduling requirements?
5. Are you licensed, bonded and insured?
6. Can you include three references with your bid?

Most building project bids will be "fixed" bids, meaning the price for a specific job is firm. Almost all phases of a building project are fixed bid.

When the extent of the work is difficult to measure until the subcontractor actually starts, the job is usually bid "time and materials". There are three subs who almost always bid time and materials: excavators, foundation subs and flatwork subs.

The excavator normally works by the hour, as they never know what they will encounter once the digging starts. For example, they could run into a rock outcropping, concealed just under the surface, that would require specialized machinery or dynamite.

The foundation subcontractor usually charges by the cubic yard of concrete, as he won't know the exact depth of the foundation until the excavation is done. Even so, you should still be able to get a fixed bid based on the plans, assuming there are no surprises with the excavation, with a per-yard figure for additional concrete.

***Never tell a sub that he was the low bidder! Instead, tell him that you want him to do the work, even though his price may be a little higher, because you think he will do a better job.***

The subcontractor who pours and finishes the concrete slab (flatwork) can give you a fixed price for the flatwork, but not for the sand or gravel used underneath the slab. Concrete contractors also do not include the cost of concrete pumping, if necessary, in their bids.

If the scope of the work is easy to understand, yet the contractor wants you to agree to a time and materials contract, watch out! This is a "red flag"—especially if other contractors are willing to give you a fixed bid for the same work. If you still decide to proceed, be sure to include a "not to exceed" price to protect yourself.

Never tell a contractor he was the low bidder! If you do, he'll be wishing he had charged more, may have a bad attitude, and may try to figure out ways to make more money, by charging you for every extra he can think of that wasn't in the contract.

Instead, tell the sub that you want him to do the work, even though his price was a little higher, because you think he will do a better job. Now you've got a happy sub on your team, whose ego has been boosted and who will do his best to surpass your expectations!

What if the subcontractor you really want to hire is the high bidder? Tell him that you would really like to hire him because you want to work with the best, but your budget is only (fill in the blank). Ask, "How can you help me get to that price?" Chances are good he'll suggest ways to make it possible. If not, he's probably too busy. You gave him an opportunity to negotiate, now you'll just have to decide if he's worth the extra money.

## Change orders

In the process of building a structure, it is almost certain there will be changes along the way. Since these changes typically fall outside of the scope of the original bids, they are usually covered by "change orders". Some builders skip the paperwork and just get a verbal okay for the cost of any changes or additions. You should not. It's a bad idea, and just another source of potential conflict. Here's a simple change order you can use to "get it in writing" and avoid future disputes or faulty memory.

**CHANGE ORDER**

We agree to make the following change:

______________________________

______________________________

______________________________

❏ Increase or ❏ decrease in job cost:

❏ Increase or ❏ decrease in time to completion:

Signature ______________________ Date ______________________

Signature ______________________ Date ______________________

After you've reviewed the bids and selected the subcontractors, it's time to set the specifics down on paper. Most contractors use a pre-printed form, but you may want to use your own contract to better protect your interest.

The contract forms produced by the American Institute of Architects are considered the best in the business, and court-tested. The best one for most small construction projects is AIA document A107, the Abbreviated Owner-Contractor Agreement Form.

You can obtain a copy of this contract form by calling the AIA National Order Center at (800) 365-2724. Read about all their contract forms at their online resource center at www.aia.org.

Here is a list of provisions that should be included in your construction contract:

- Date of the agreement
- Name and address of both owner and contractor
- Contractor's license/registration number
- Location of the job site
- Plans or other drawings should be referenced and made a part of the contract
- Who is responsible for obtaining the necessary permits and inspection approvals?
- Start and finish dates for the work covered by the contract
- Who is responsible for materials required to complete the work?
- Stipulated pricing for changes and additions. For example: *Materials cost not to exceed cost plus ten percent. Labor not to exceed $45 per hour.*
- Cleanup requirements at the job site. For example: When the work is completed, the job site will be "broom clean" and all waste and debris will be disposed of in compliance with local ordinances.
- A price and payment schedule for work completed. For a smaller project like a barn or garage, most subcontractors will simply be paid upon completion, subject to any required inspections of their work, such as an electrical inspection. If the project will take place in phases over time, pay a percentage based on the amount of work completed in each phase.

Most construction contracts use the phrase "substantial completion". What this means is the project is finished and the building is usable for the purpose for which it was intended. If, for example, the roofing is not installed, the building is not substantially completed. If the Dutch door latches are back-ordered, and your contractor can't install them, pay up!

If a contractor asks you for a substantial up-front payment or deposit, or a large payment for materials before they have been delivered, or much work has been done, beware! This should be a large red flag. Reputable contractors have credit accounts with their suppliers and should not need to get money up-front from you to pay for materials.

Contractors are typically billed at the end of the month by the lumberyard or other materials supplier. They then have 10 days to pay the bill. If a sub asks for a substantial payment to cover materials, ask to see the actual bills. Then write a check payable to both the contractor and supplier, or offer to pay the materials supplier directly. Both of these methods allow the supplier to get paid immediately, lessening the chances of a materials lien on your property later.

• Waiver of mechanic's liens.

A mechanic's lien is a legal claim against your property from a supplier of labor or materials. This worst-case scenario actually happened to an unfortunate neighbor recently. Let's say you pay a contractor or subcontractor who purchases materials that are delivered to and used on your building project.

The contractor gave you a low bid, which didn't quite cover the cost of labor and materials. By the time the contractor figured out his mistake, he spent the money and never paid for the materials. He files for bankruptcy and skips town. Two weeks later, you receive notice that a materials' lien has been filed on your property!

Here's a provision you can add to your agreement with subs to address this common problem:

*"Contractor shall provide to owner, before payment, acknowledgement of payment from each supplier or subcontractor for all materials, equipment and labor. Upon final payment, the contractor shall provide waivers or releases of payment from all suppliers and subcontractors."*

• A provision acknowledging the contractor has met the insurance requirements for your state, typically a minimum of worker's compensation, liability insurance and a contractor's bond.

In addition, the agreement should make it clear you are hiring an independent contractor, not an employee. Here's an example:

*Contractor represents himself as an independent contractor, and shall be solely responsible for the payment of unemployment insurance, Social Security, state and federal income taxes and any other taxes on the payments made under this agreement. Contractor also shall have no right or claim for any worker's compensation, medical, or other benefits for the work performed under this agreement."*

• You expect anyone working on your building project to work safely. It's important to include this in your agreement.

*"The contractor shall at all times take reasonable precautions to protect the person and property of others, on or adjacent to the work site, from damage, loss or injury."*

- Make sure disputes between the owner and contractor will be settled through arbitration or mediation, each a much less costly process than a lawsuit.

*"All claims and disputes between the parties that relate to this agreement shall be resolved by arbitration or mediation, unless the parties mutually agree to resolve them by other means."*

- If everything goes totally bonkers, make sure you have a termination clause in your agreement. For example:

*"If good cause exists, owner may, by written notice to contractor, terminate this agreement. Contractor shall stop work immediately upon receipt of a notice of termination. All disputes over payments, due and owing, shall be resolved in arbitration or mediation."*

## How to help your subcontractors

Having a clearly written agreement, spelling out all the details of what you and your contractor/subcontractor expect of each other, will go a long way towards preventing problems from occurring.

Even a well-written agreement can leave a lot of latitude in how to interpret it. For example, if the contract calls for payment in full on completion of framing, do you pay the day after the framing passed inspection, or do you drag your feet for a week?

It's common practice in the building industry to practice a variation of the Golden Rule, called ***"He who has the gold, rules."*** Whatever the reason, the owner chooses not to pay exactly as agreed. The net effect is that the subcontractors immediately lose any respect they may have for you, as they try to figure out how to pay *their* bills.

So remember the original Golden Rule, ***"Do unto others, as you would have others do unto you."*** Treat your subcontractors as the decent human beings they are, pay as agreed, and move on to the next phase.

Here are a few other simple things you can do to make your sub's life a little easier, and in turn, yours, too.

- Try to visit the building site at least once, and preferably twice a day. So much can happen in the course of one day, on a construction project. Your job is to be there to make the necessary decisions, answer questions, check the work to make sure it's being done correctly and on schedule, and make sure the subs have whatever they need to do good work.

- Make sure each sub has a daytime phone number where you can be reached if there are any problems or questions.

- A basic fax machine, mentioned earlier, is an essential communications tool, when something needs to be in writing.

- If you don't have existing sanitation facilities close by the job site, rent a portable toilet for the duration of the project.

- Make sure the job site is kept clean and safe. In addition to requiring each sub to clean up after their debris, you should plan on pitching in with a broom, too. Most subs will leave the job site in the same condition they found it, whether it was clean or a mess.

- Provide a good all-weather road to the job site. A few yards of gravel, or crushed rock, can turn a muddy mess into a clean driveway. If the driveway doesn't extend all the way to the building, use straw to keep the path drier and free of mud.

- All contractors appreciate special treats, like fresh baked cookies or soft drinks. My "Friday Special" was hot pizza delivered to the building site just in time for lunch. Sharing lunch provides a good time to review the week's progress and keep in closer touch with the work crew.

- So everyone on the building site has access to the construction plans, leave a set in a safe place and tell everyone how to find them. In addition, building inspectors often require that an approved set be available at all times on the building site.

# Common Mistakes

I have a hunch that Murphy's Law originated with the building trades, where the potential for problems, large and small, occurs every day. From the day the building takes shape on the drawing board, until the last nail is hammered home, people will do dumb things.

Fortunately for you, the owner-builder, most mistakes can be avoided with a dose of common sense, proper planning, and knowing the solutions to the most common building mistakes outlined in this chapter.

> ***"If anything can go wrong, it probably will."***
> ***—Murphy's Law***

If you follow the suggestions, plan well, and keep a positive attitude about your building project, you'll do better than the other 99 percent of owner-builders, who were unprepared to deal with the challenges of managing such a project.

*Don't Sweat the Small Stuff,* the title of a recent best-selling book, truly applies to construction, where lots of small stuff goes wrong each and every day. Just remember to focus on getting the "big stuff" right, and you'll be okay.

In my 30 years of working with owner-builders, I've noticed that their mistakes consistently tend to fall into five areas.

1. Costs are underestimated. Or worse yet, there is no project budget at all!

2. Owner-builders try to do too much of the actual construction work themselves, when their time, energy and skills would be better used to manage the building project.

3. Problems with subcontractors, ranging from no shows to work not completed. Contractors who do show up can be late to start, slow to finish and/or do sloppy work. If they get paid early, you may never see them again, whether the work was done or not.

4. Owner-builders tend to rush a project, rather than taking adequate time to plan ahead and do everything well. As the saying goes, "There's never time to do it right, but always time to do it over."

5. Get it in writing! I'm convinced that the majority of the big problems that develop in the construction process arise from not putting everything in writing, from the basic specifications to the agreements with the subcontractors.

Let's take a look at specific problems in these five areas, together with solutions for each problem.

> ***"Fall seven times, get up eight.."***
> ***—Japanese proverb***

### Where did all the money go?

To avoid underestimating the cost of your building project—or worse yet, running out of money before the building is finished—plan ahead. Use the forms provided in the back of the this book to pin down accurate estimates for all phases of your building project, then stick to them. Establish a budget, and stick to that, also.

I've seen too many building projects slip into financial trouble because of seemingly small additions to the budget. It's so easy to say, "It's only $500 extra. We can surely afford it." But, do it a dozen times, and there goes the budget, and probably your contingency reserve fund, too!

For the same reason, avoid making design changes after the plans are completed and you've accepted bids from subcontractors. The farther along your building project, the more expensive changes become.

### Do you really want to do it all?

At least once a month, I get a letter and photos from a customer who cut his own trees, brought in a mobile mini-sawmill to turn the logs into rough-cut lumber, and then built every bit of the building himself—usually for a fraction of the normal cost of construction. Yet, I would never recommend that path for most owner-builders, because it's so time-consuming.

Most of us have to balance our time versus our money. We need to choose the phases of construction to participate in, based on the amount of free time we have, our skills and the complexity of the work.

Be realistic about your skills. If you've never poured concrete before, a 10-cubic-yard foundation may not be the best place to learn! Sometimes it's better to hire a pro for critical phases, such as the foundation or the electrical wiring, for example.

Owner-builders often get so involved in the actual physical work that they neglect the equally important work of managing the project.

One technique that allows you to save money while you learn—as well as avoiding potentially serious mistakes—is to work beside the subs of your choice, doing the phases of construction you want to learn more about.

For example, except for the smallest barn or garage, framing the exterior shell requires two, or more, people just because of the size of some of the components. Try tilting up a 20-foot barn wall by yourself to see what I mean.

Most subcontractors will discount their bid a bit in exchange for your labor as an unskilled "grunt". You'll learn a lot, and have the hands-on satisfaction of participating in yet another phase of your building project.

## Problems with subcontractors

It's been my experience that most subcontractors are reasonable folks, who really want to do their best on your building project. They bring valuable skills and knowledge, and expect to be treated fairly.

Like most relationships, problems can develop and damage or destroy your ability to work together. The good news is that most problems can be traced back to a mistake made early in the relationship—a miscommunication, or not enough detail in an agreement, for example. Recognize them early, and they can be corrected before they can do any harm.

When I talk to owner-builders about subcontractors, there are eight common problems that seem to show up over and over again. The good news: Each problem has a solution.

## Subs are late

This is the most common complaint of both owner-builders and professional builders, because of the "domino theory". When the excavator doesn't show up when scheduled, it affects the schedule of the foundation sub, then the framing sub, and on down the line of subcontractors.

Because we live in an imperfect world, you'll never completely eliminate this problem. Check your construction schedule in Chapter 5. You'll notice that the subs asked for XX days advanced notice. Try calling your subs once a week to update them on the schedule. Ask, "How's your schedule looking?" Then call again, a day or two before their scheduled start date, to remind them. It's also a good idea to tell them you'll meet them at the building site to go over the job with them before they start.

One incentive, guaranteed to get a sub's attention, is a cash bonus for early completion. You can include it in a written agreement, or dangle it as bait, if your sub is a no-show on the start date.

### Subs never show up

If you've done a good job screening your subs, this will almost never be a problem. When it is, there's usually a reasonable explanation, such as a family/medical emergency. Don't get upset until you have all the facts. Then, if there's no hope of getting the sub on the job soon enough to suit you, call the other bidders and see if they can work you into their schedule.

### Subs don't finish the work

It's not uncommon for subcontractors, especially the smaller ones, to have two or more builders call and try to schedule them for the same time period. If the sub expects to do future jobs for the builder who wants him the same week you do, guess what happens to your schedule?

Most subs will do their best not to hold up a project, even if it means working mornings at one job site and afternoons at another to keep both happy. If your schedule allows it, be patient. If not, remember that cash talks, and an early-completion bonus is a powerful motivator!

### Subs do incorrect or sloppy work

Miscommunication is always the reason work doesn't get done the way you expected. Meet the subcontractor on the building site before they begin the work, and discuss the work they will be doing. Make sure they have accurate, up-to-date plans and specifications—and that they understand them.

Visit the building site every day to keep track of the work. This allows you to catch any potential problems before they become big problems. Almost all subs have cell phones to keep in touch, so make sure they have your number to call in case they have questions or problems.

### Subs want more money

Be sure that you have a signed agreement with each subcontractor, before the work starts, that spells out the dollar amount, the payment schedule, and the exact scope of the work.

Any changes must be written up on a change order (see the Construction Forms in the back of this book) and signed by both parties before the work proceeds. Some contractors like to get paid cash "off the books" to avoid taxes. Don't do it. Write a check to cover payments, so you have a record of what was paid and when it was paid.

### Sub doesn't finish the job because you paid him too much, too soon!

A friend's recent experience brought this one home. She hired a carpenter to build her entire barn, including a Victorian cupola destined to be the finest cupola in the entire county.

The project moved along slowly with just one carpenter and an occasional helper. One day, with the roof sheathed in only plywood and a giant hole cut where the grand cupola was to rest, the carpenter told her that he was about to lose his house to the bank because he was behind in his payments. She took pity on him, and gave him the final payment for the barn construction, even though it was nowhere near finished.

Eighteen months later…still no roofing or cupola. The carpenter left town and the owner doesn't have an extra $4,000 to hire someone else to complete the project.

Moral of this story – remember the "Golden Rule of Construction":

***He who has the gold rules.***

Never pay for work until it's satisfactorily completed. If you do, the subcontractor has no incentive to finish and you have lost your leverage.

### Subcontractor or supplier places lien on your property

Be sure to specify in all your subs' contracts that lien releases, or waivers from the suppliers, will be provided by the sub. This will protect you. Also, unless you're paying for the materials and the sub is just providing labor, don't sign for materials being delivered to the building site. If you sign for deliveries, you may be held accountable for payment. Another common safeguard is to make the check payable to both the subcontractor and the materials supplier. This gives the supplier a chance to collect for materials before the contractor spends the money on other things.

While most problems with subcontractors result from a mistake, or a series of mistakes, early in the building process, they are often compounded by the owner-builder's attitude. Subs are human, just like you and I, and would rather be told what a good job they're doing than be yelled at.

One solution I've found in dealing with subs is to ask questions, rather than making demands. You'll come across as concerned, not confrontational. For example, *"I noticed your crew framed two window openings in the north wall. Wasn't there just one shown on the plans?"* That's more effective than, *"Get over here now! Those stupid framers just screwed up again!"*

Always try to give your subs the benefit of the doubt. Assume they are doing the best job they can. A building project is a cooperative event, and a positive attitude on your part will help keep it that way.

If, in spite of your heroic efforts, things turn ugly, remember that you're entitled to get what the written agreement with your contractor spells out. That's what you're paying for. There is no reason for you to compromise your rights just to make your sub happy!

Even when everyone is doing their best to maintain a positive working relationship, mistakes happen. There are three basic solutions to most mistakes.

1. The problem can be ignored. (The electrician put the extra receptacle on the west wall instead of the north wall, but it will work just as well.)
2. The subcontractor fixes it for free. (The plumber goofed, and hot water is coming out of the outside hose bib.)
3. The owner pays to have it fixed. (You meant to change the plans to show the loft window moved 6 feet to the left, but forgot.)

These simple solutions work best with small mistakes. When the stakes are higher, in dollars or frustration, you may need to go to the next level of dispute resolution. At this level, there are still three basic methods used to resolve problems.

## Lawsuits

In a lawsuit, the parties involved hire lawyers to present their side before a judge, who makes a final binding decision. Lawsuits are a poor way to resolve most construction disputes because they are so expensive and time-consuming for both parties. It's often said that the lawyers are the only winners in a lawsuit.

## Binding arbitration

In an arbitration, the parties involved hire lawyers to present their side before a professional in the disputed field, building construction for example. The arbitrator might be an architect or a construction manager. After hearing both sides of the case, the arbitrator, acting as judge, makes a legally-binding decision.

The advantage of arbitration is that it is private, quicker than a lawsuit, and less expensive. The disadvantage is there is no appeal process. The arbitrator's decision is final.

## Mediation

In mediation, the parties involved use a trained professional mediator to guide them towards a mutually acceptable settlement. While mediation is not as formal as going to court or arbitration, it generally follows a formal six step structure designed to move the parties towards settlement.

If you've tried and failed to settle your dispute directly with a supplier or subcontractor, mediation may be the most efficient way to reach resolution. Compared to a lawsuit—or even arbitration—mediation is cheap, confidential, fair and quick.

All parties to the dispute must agree to mediate, so it's important to mention either arbitration or mediation in any written agreement. If it's not mentioned in the agreement, and one party refuses, the case cannot be mediated. (More on contracts in Chapter Eight.)

For a more complete explanation of these three methods of conflict resolution, go to the informative legal website, www.nolo.com. Click on "lawcenter", then "FAQ" to find out more about arbitration and mediation. And be sure to read the latest lawyer jokes at the site!

# Gable Roof Barn Plans

In the pages that follow are basic construction drawings for twelve barn designs that range from under 300 square feet to over 1800 square feet. These designs have been built from Florida to Alaska—on quarter-acre suburban lots and thousand acre ranches.

The barn designs are arranged in the chapters that follow by roof style, then size. In this chapter, you'll find gable roof barns, the most common roof style. A gable roof has two sloping sides that meet at a center ridge. A low pitch (slope) is common on single story barns. A steeply-pitched gable roof can allow a generous attic space, and shed winter snows better than a lower pitched roof.

Chapter 11 features several gambrel roof barns. The gambrel, often called a "Dutch" barn, has long been popular because the steeply sloping sides allow more room in the loft than a gable roof. A gambrel roof is a combination of two gable roofs—one with a steep slope—the upper with a more normal slope.

Chapter 12 features "monitor" roof barns, so called because of the raised center "monitor" section. Often called a "Western" barn, the style features a center gable roof over the monitor portion and shed roofs over the two lower sides.

When we send a complete set of plans for one of these barns to a builder or owner-builder, we assume that it will be modified to meet the specific needs of the owner and the building site. It may be a simple modification, such as adding or moving a window or door, or it can be as complex as stretching the length to provide more stalls inside.

In many cases, the changes were so extensive that the plans had to be completely redrawn before construction could start. When major changes are a possibility, it doesn't always make sense to purchase complete plans when they may not be usable as originally drawn. Being able to see the actual construction drawings of the barn can help the owner and the builder understand the structural components that will be affected by any modifications to the basic plans.

Each basic plan includes the floor plans, a front and side elevation, a structural cross-section, and a roof framing plan. If there is a second floor or loft, a floor framing plan is also included. These plans will give you the essential information to develop your own personalized barn design.

If you are not making major changes to one of these barn designs, you may want to purchase the full set of construction plans, which are drawn to standard architectural scale on 11" x 17" sheets, and include, in addition to the drawings shown in this book, a foundation plan, supplemental detail drawings, two additional elevations, a specifications sheet, and a complete materials list to take to the lumberyard. You'll find an order blank in the back of this book, or you can go to our web site, www.homesteaddesign.com.

We strongly recommend that you consult with qualified design or building professionals in your area. They can ensure that the structure you build is suitable for local conditions, codes and your intended use.

# The Concord

If you have a limited budget or yard space, the Concord could be just the right size barn for you. It can be built as a garden shed with an attached greenhouse, a compact garage and shop, or as a mini-barn with an attached tack room. A 200 square foot storage loft provides extra room. The height of the Concord is 16'9".

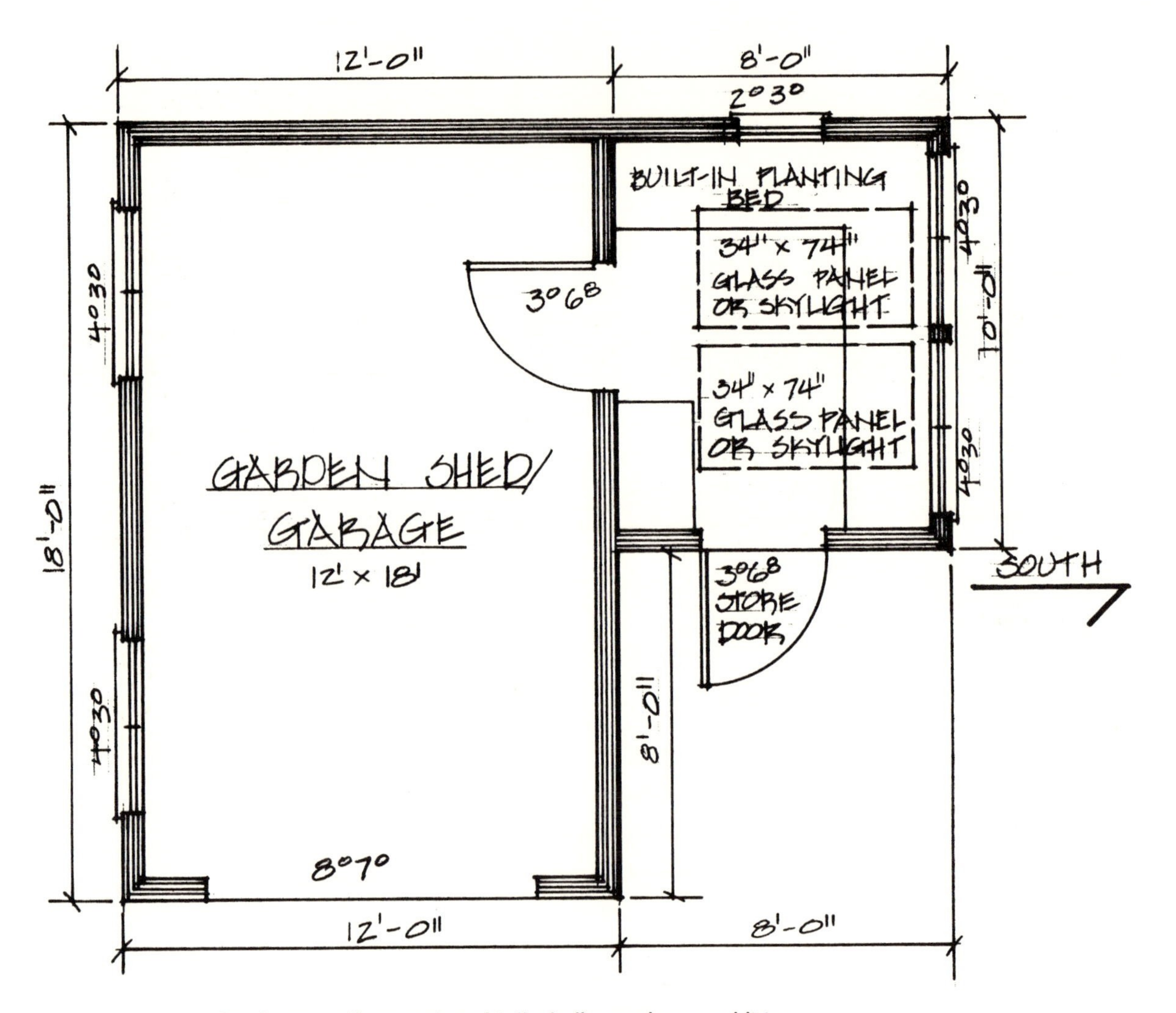


Gardeners will appreciate this "solar" greenhouse addition.

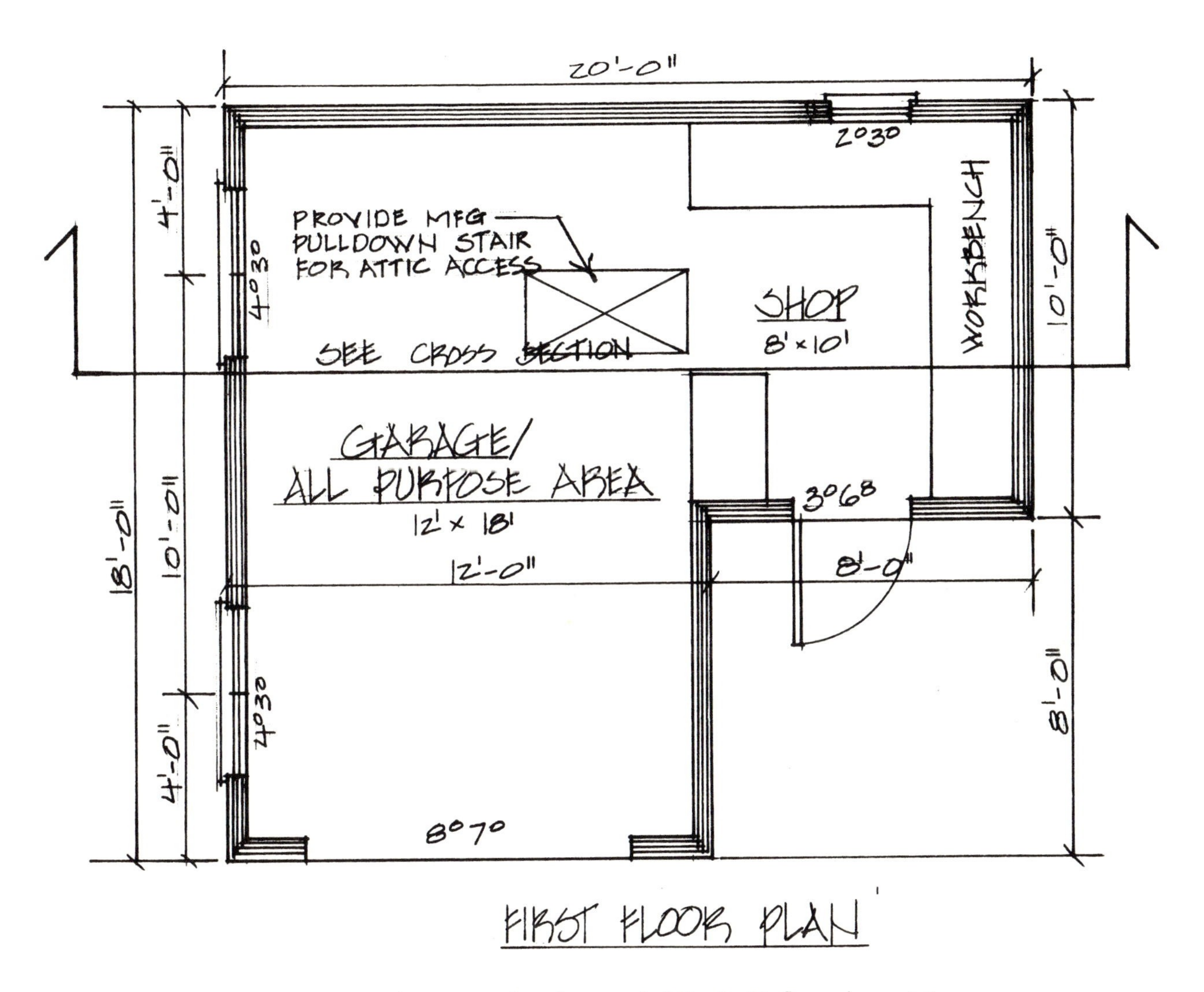


A compact shop for your hobbies in this floor plan variation.

An overhead door can be substituted for the barn-style door.

The South elevation of the greenhouse version of the Concord.

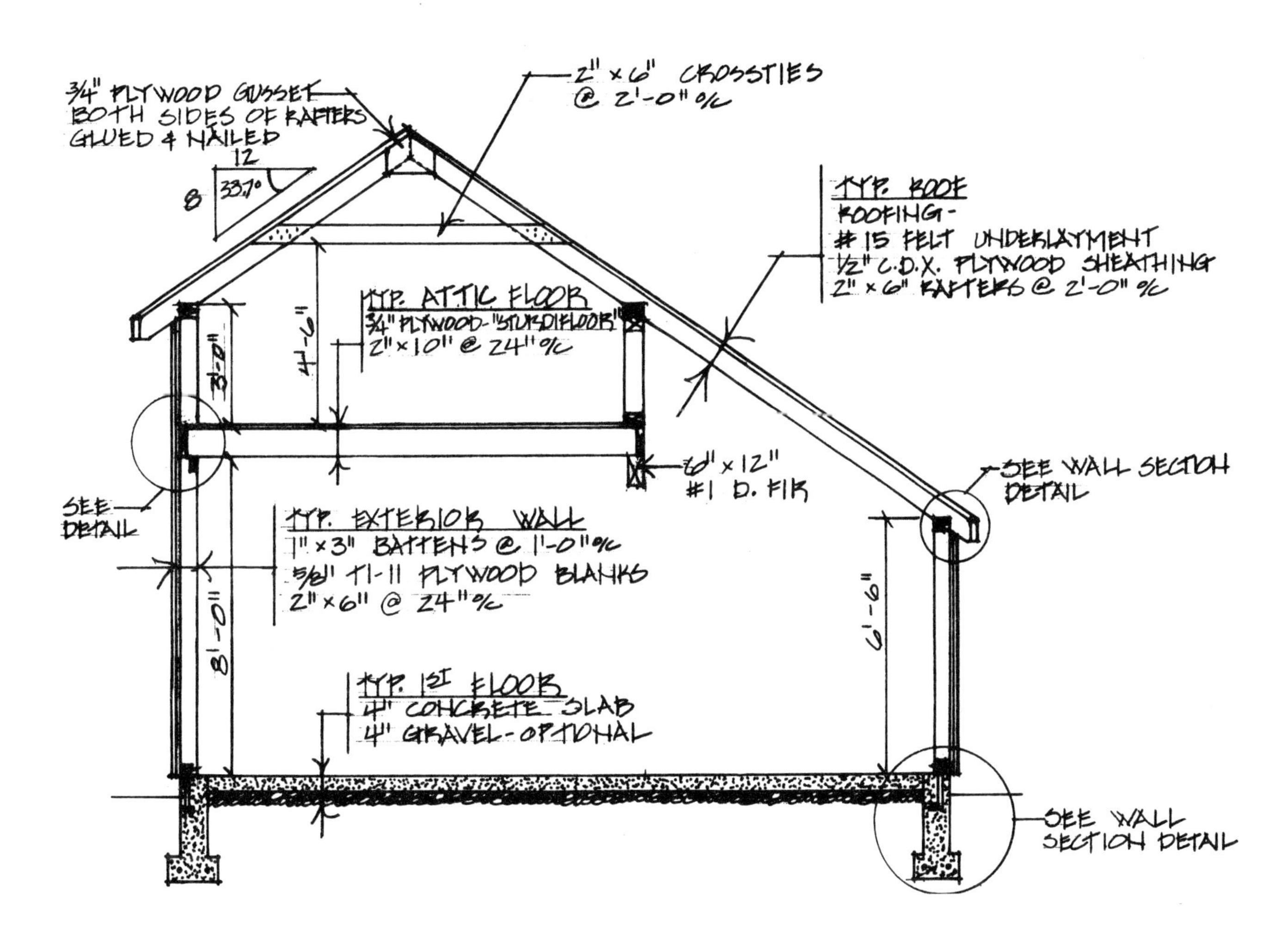


This "x-ray" view reveals the structural components of the Concord.

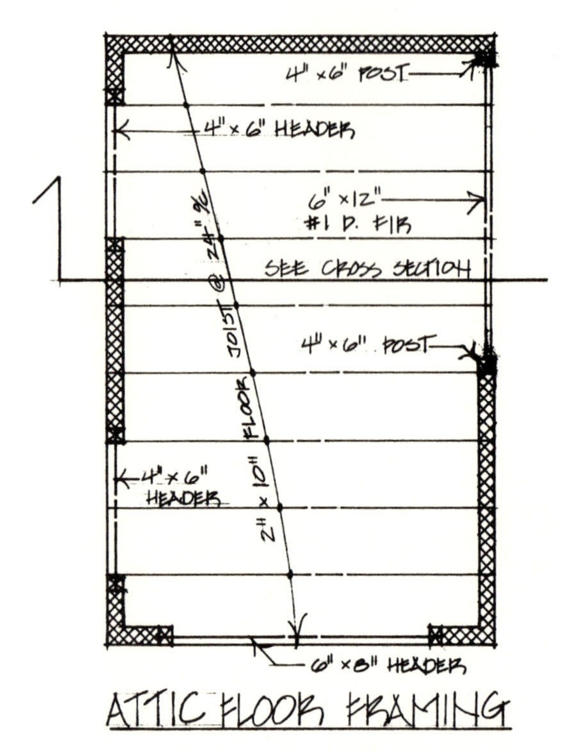


Sturdy attic floor framing allows ample storage capacity.

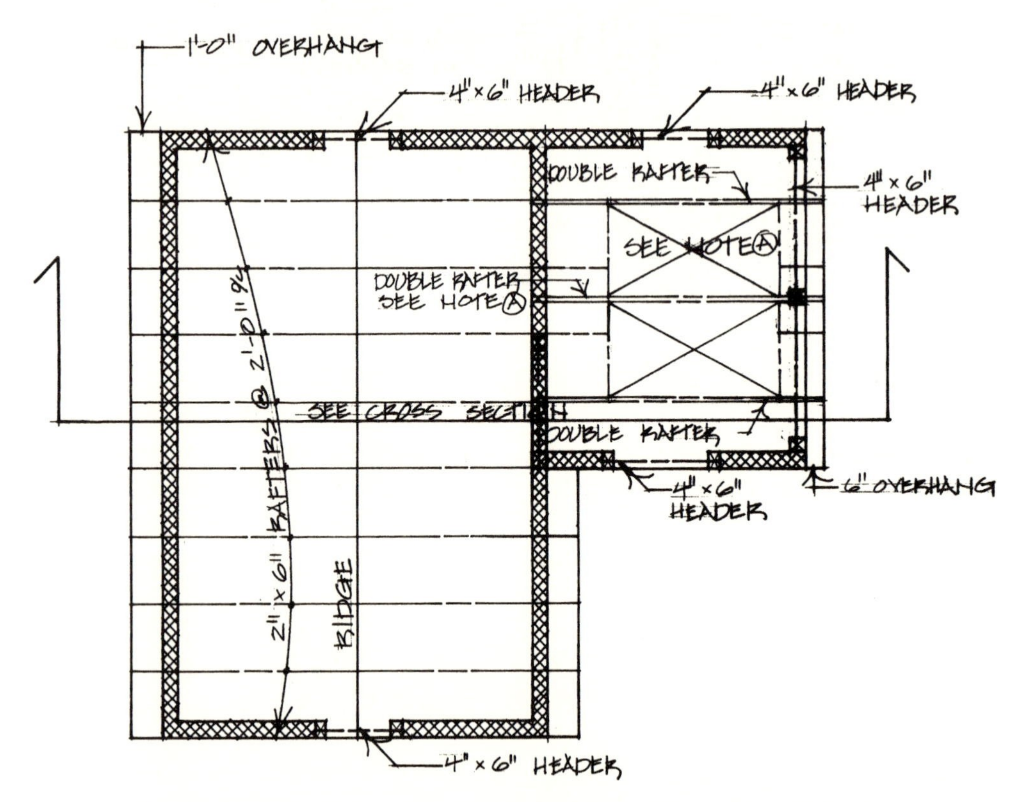


2 x 6 rafters handle average snow loads. Increasing the rafters to 2 x 8s allows room for R21 insulation and handles an 80 pound snow load.

# The Pilchuck

The classic simplicity of this compact barn will fit right in on your country property, with economical construction costs a bonus. A full storage loft provides additional room. A wing, or two, built now or later, can more than double the usable space affordably. Three floor plan options allow you to tailor this plan to your needs. The Pilchuck is 21'6" tall.

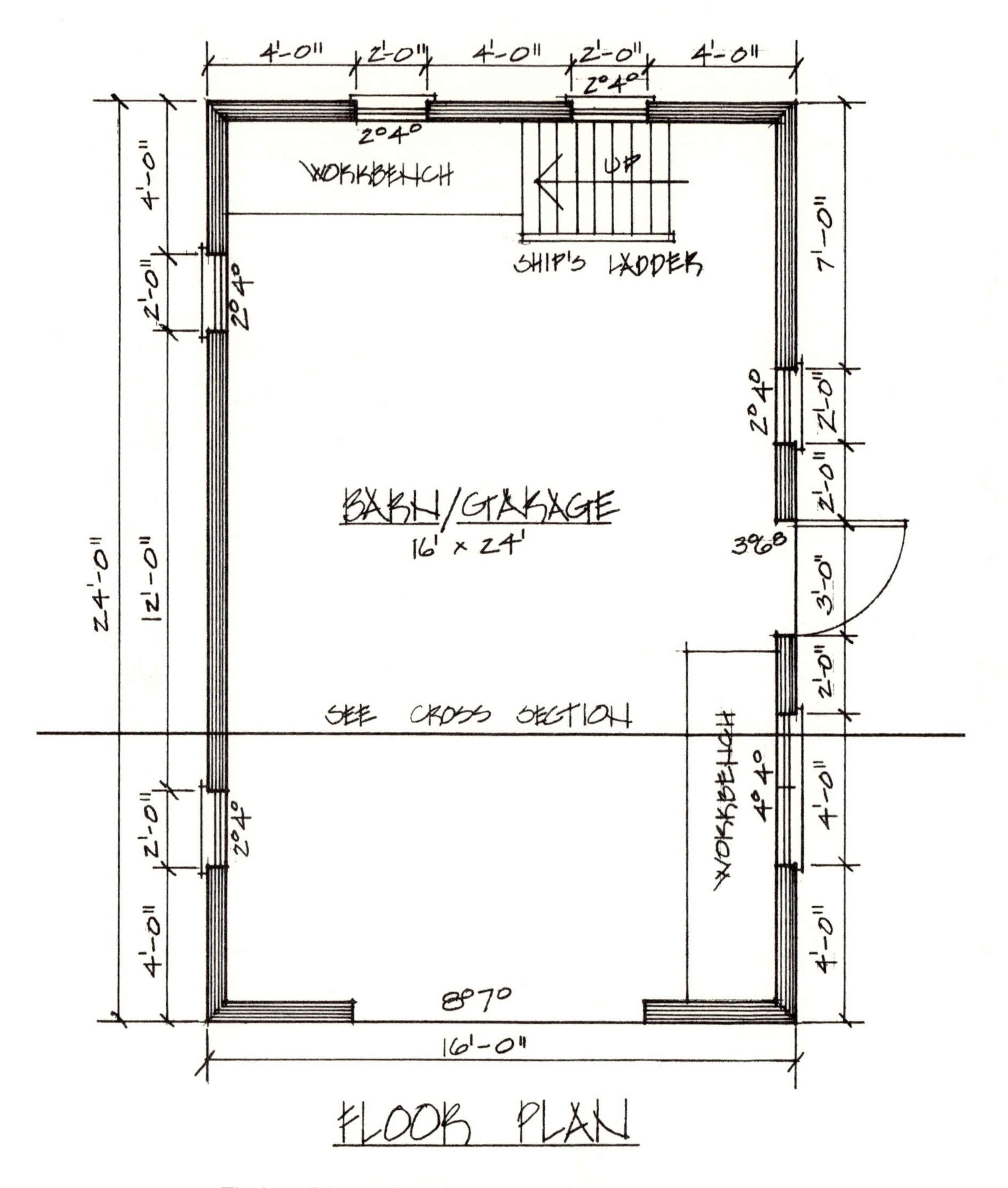


The basic Pilchuck floor plan provides almost 400 square feet of usable space on each level.

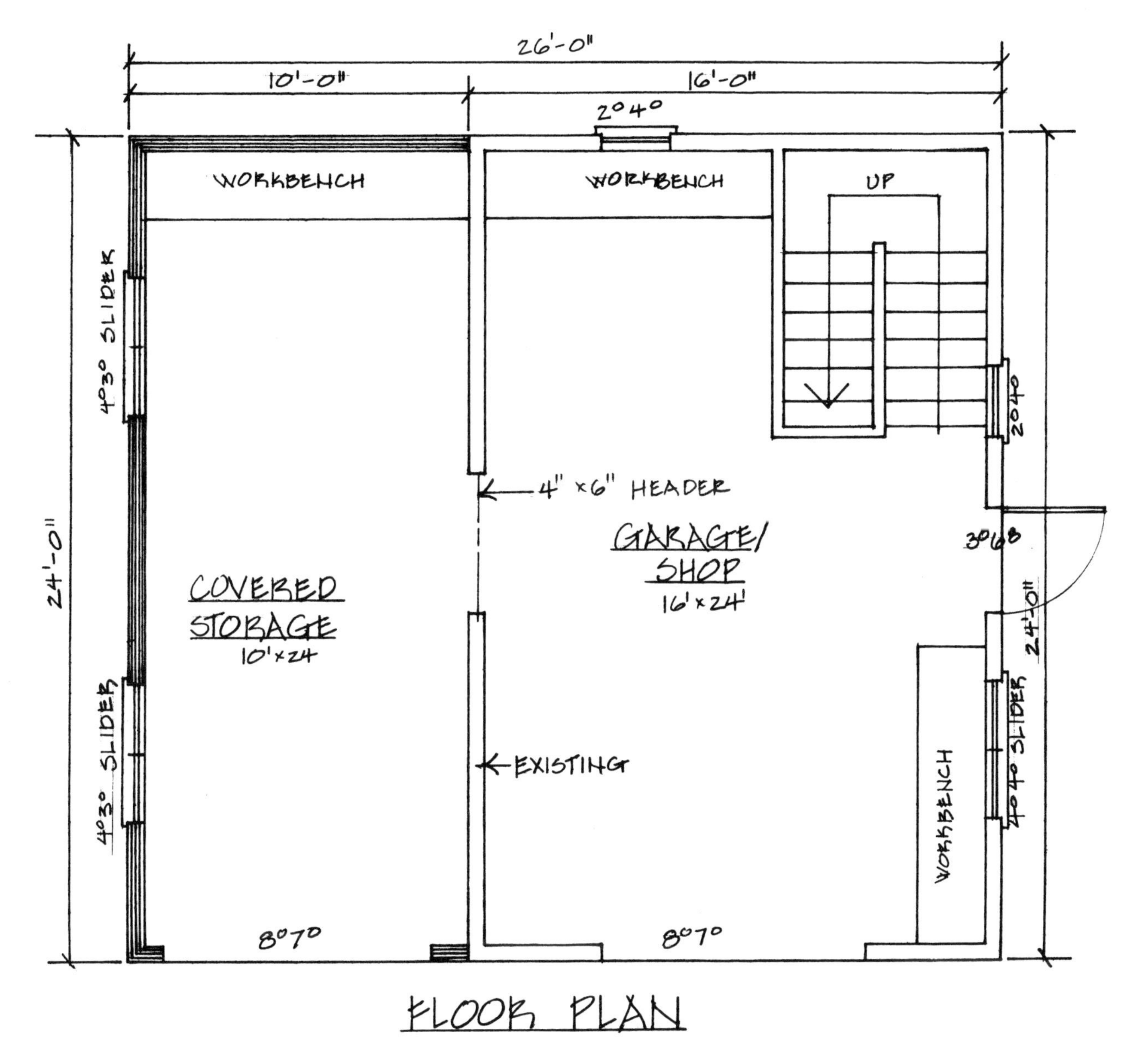


Adding a wing provides an additional 240 square feet of room.

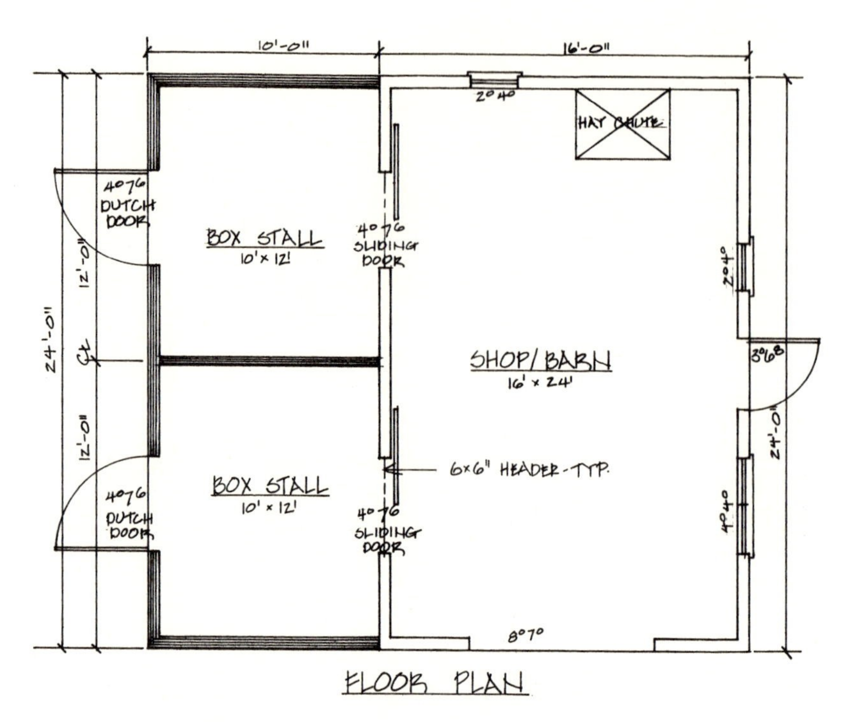


Two stalls can be added to the basic barn.
A similar wing on the opposite side provides a total of 4 stalls.

A window can be substituted for the loft doors if desired.

The storage/garage wing with matching doors.

A window over the workbench and a window to light the stairwell.

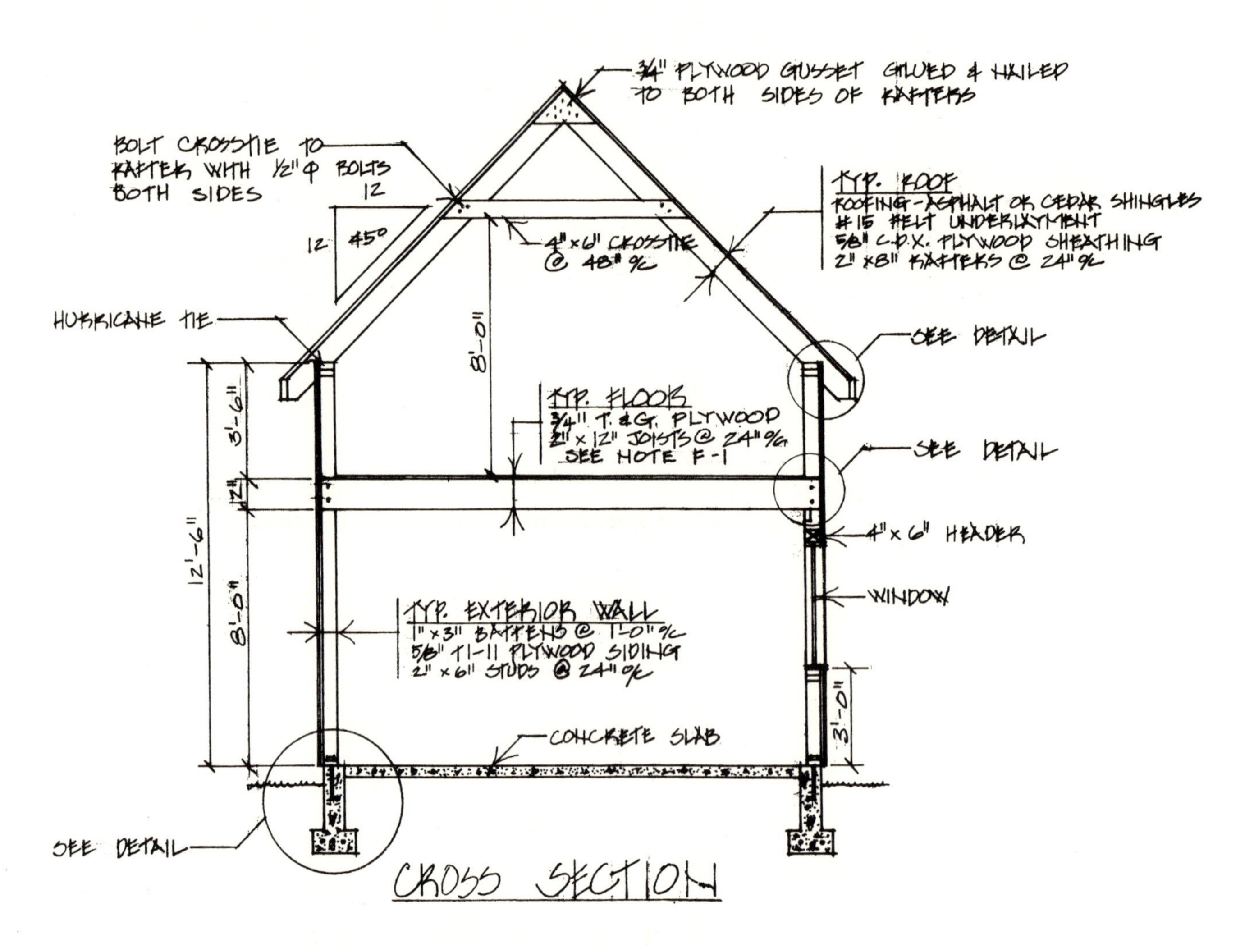


For standing headroom in the full loft, increase the knee-wall height by 2 feet.

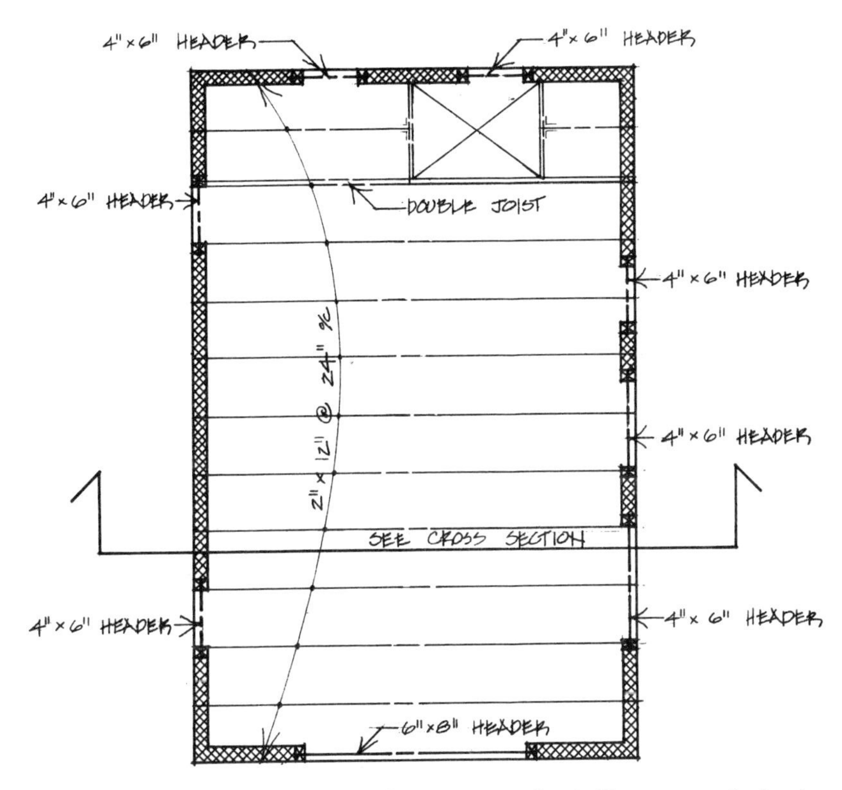


The loft floor is designed to support normal attic storage loads. To increase the load capacity by 50 percent, space the loft floor joists on 16 inch centers.

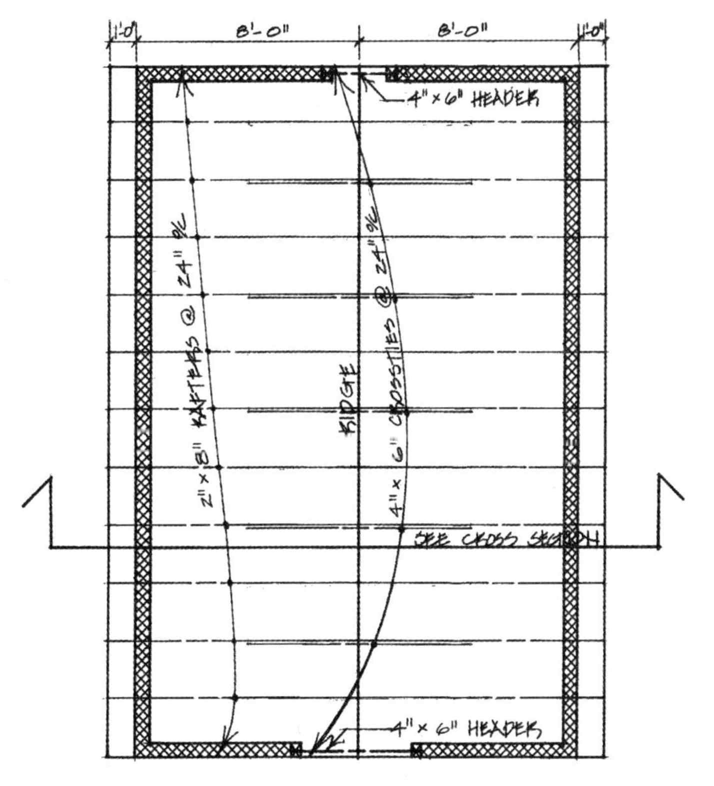


2 x 8 rafters allow room for R21 insulation, if desired, and provide support for a snow load of over 80 pounds per square foot.

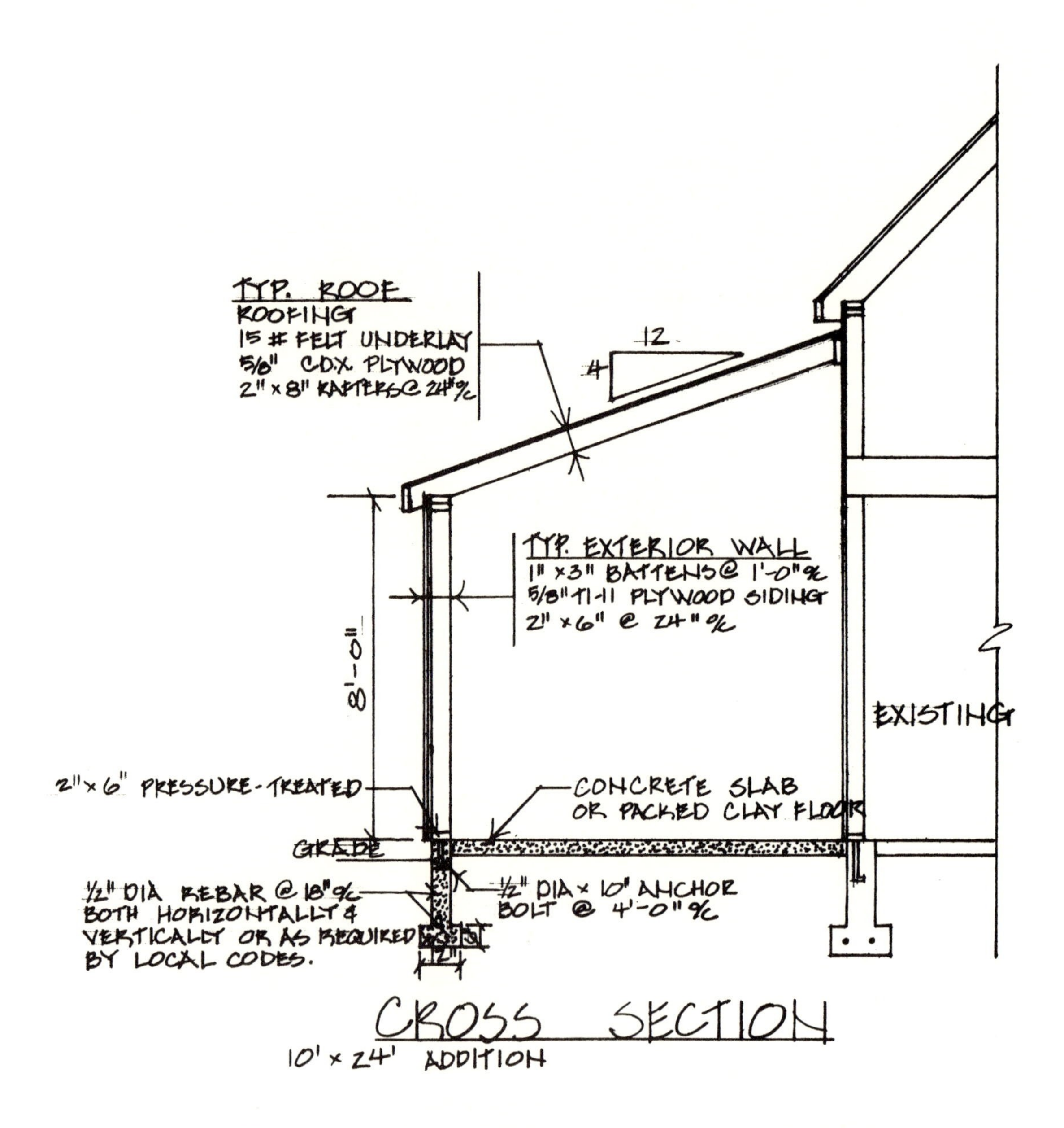


The expansion wings provide inexpensive space because they utilize the structure of the "core" barn for support.

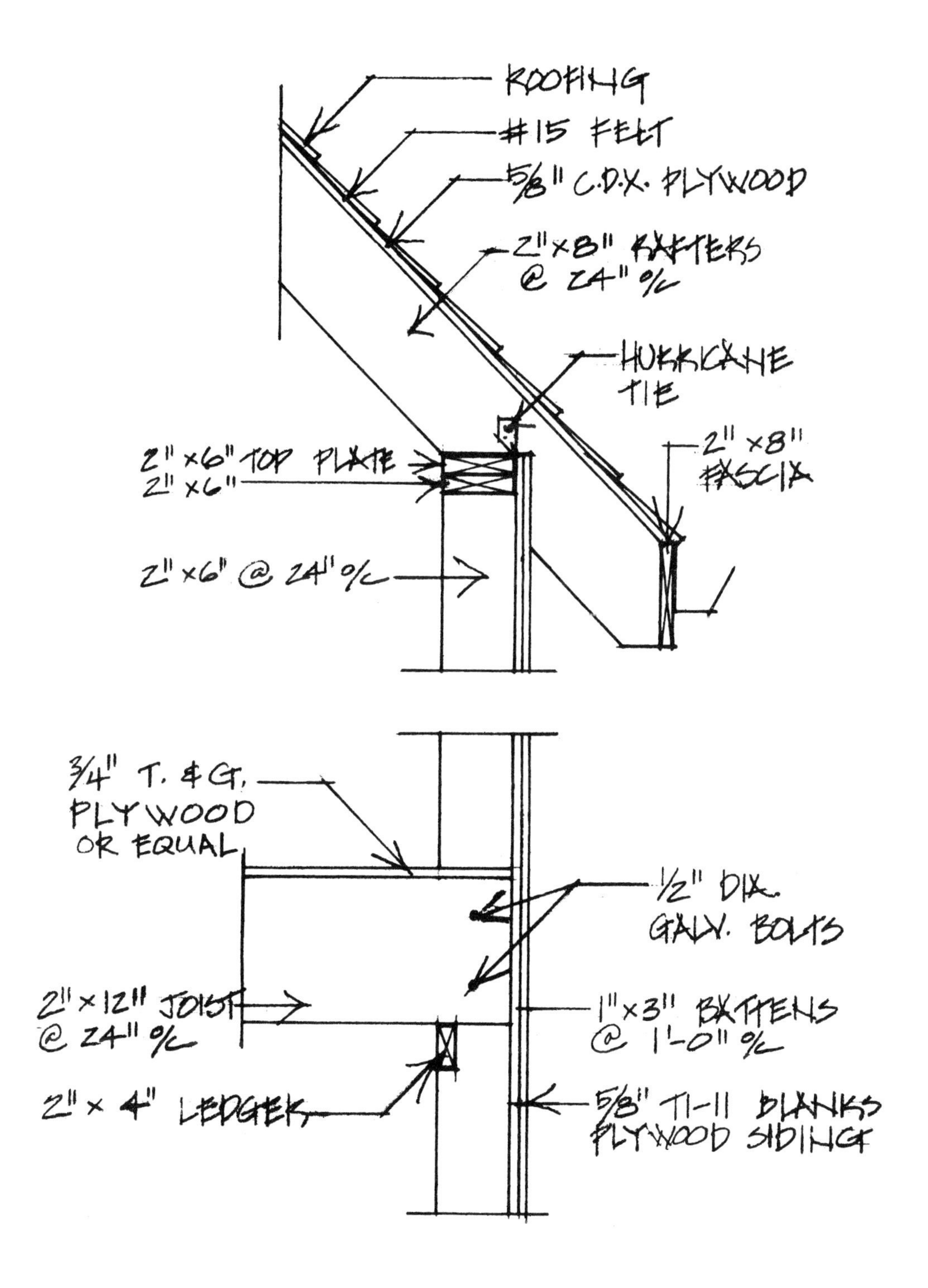


"Balloon" framing, with continuous wall studs, provides structural rigidity to the exterior walls.

## The Prescott

This economical pole frame barn gives you the flexibility to start with just a one-stall structure. Then add another stall—or a tack and feed room later. A modular design allows the addition of two more stalls in the future. The height of the Prescott is 15'6".

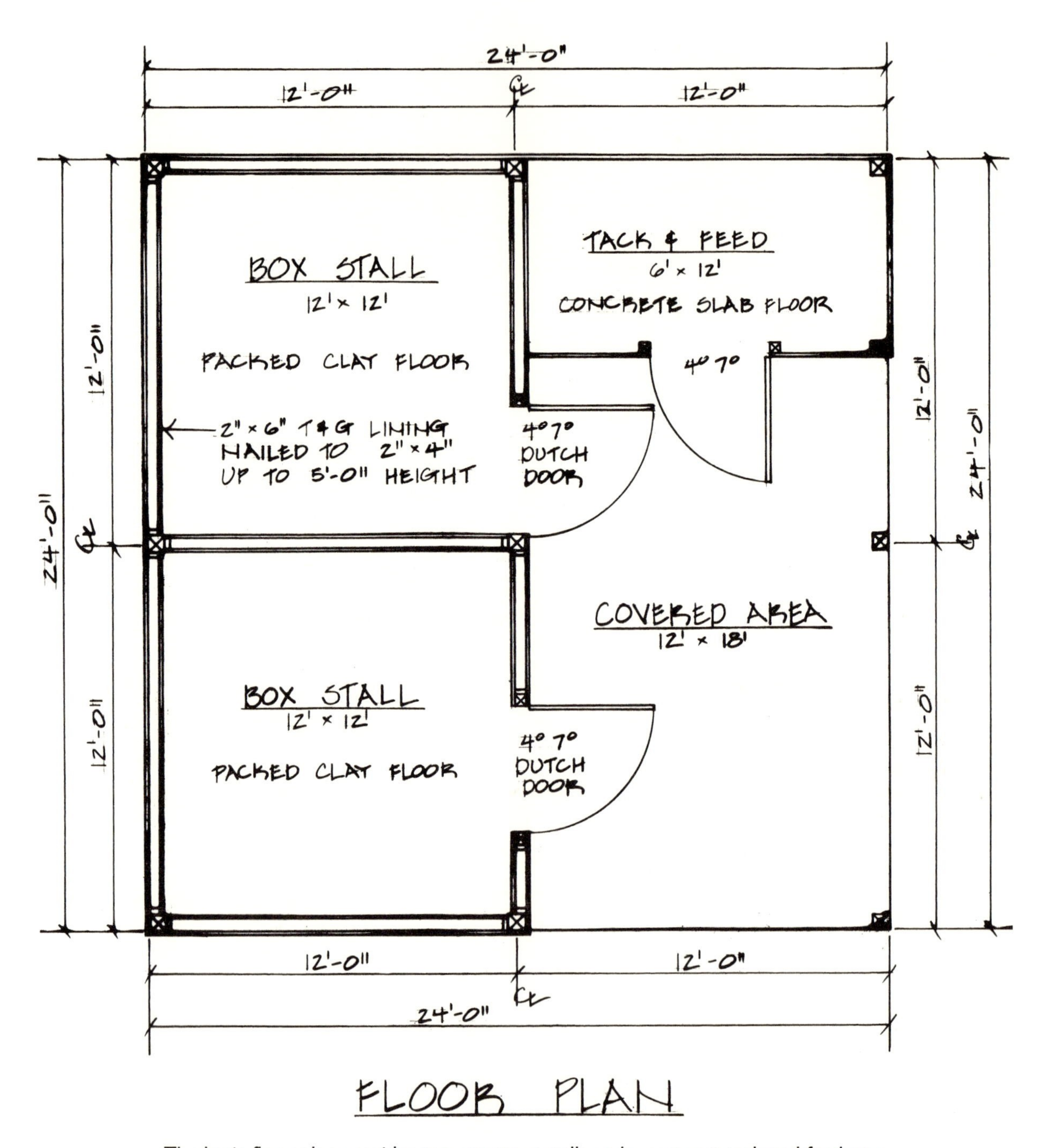


The basic floor plan provides two generous stalls and a compact tack and feed area.

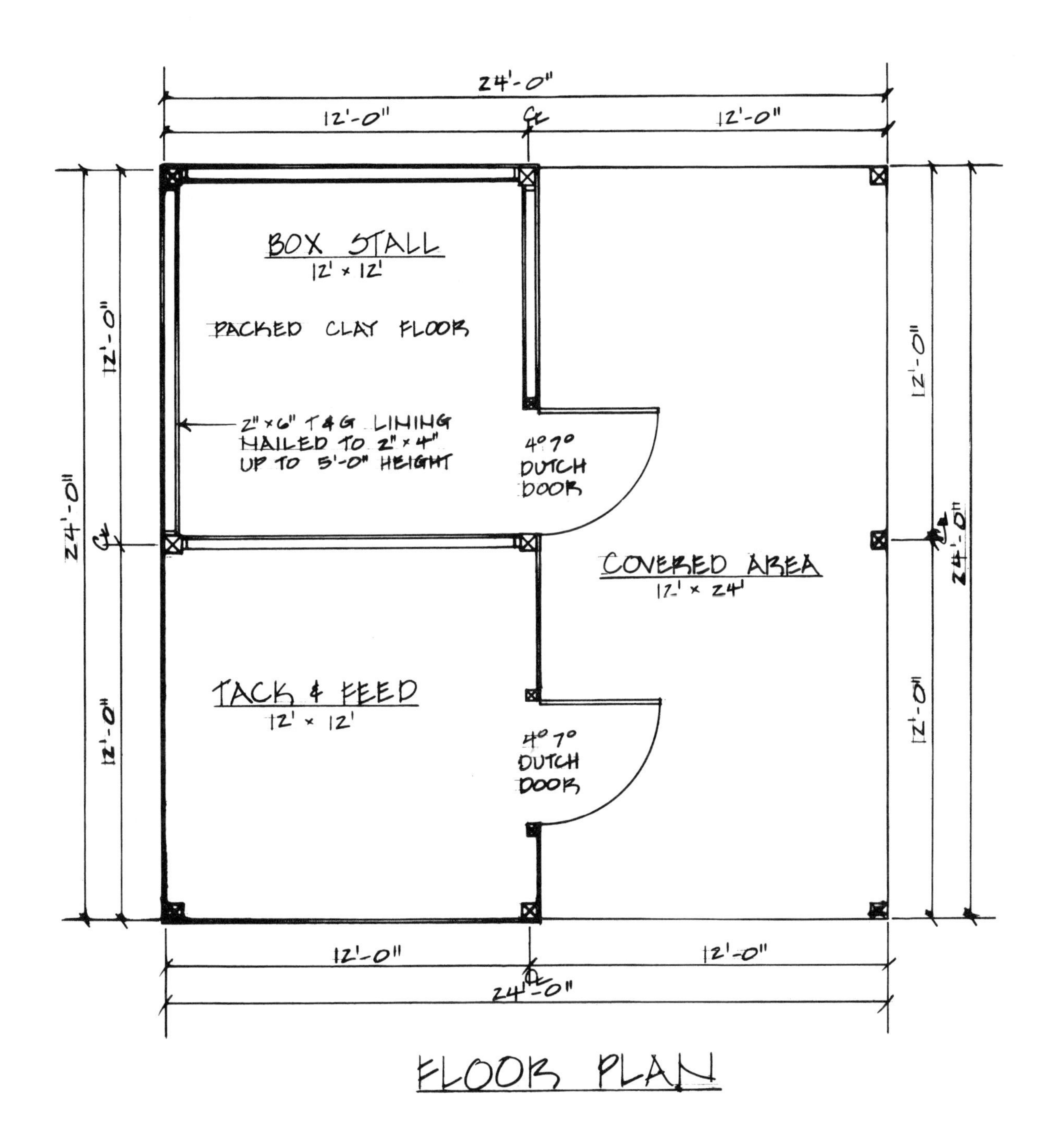


The single-stall floor plan is ideal for those with only one horse, and features a larger tack and feed area and a large covered area.

FRONT ELEVATION

The Prescott barn features economical board-and-batten siding.
A Dutch door is shown for the feed and tack room.

SIDE ELEVATION

Both stalls are shown with Dutch doors that can provide
improved ventilation when the top half is opened.

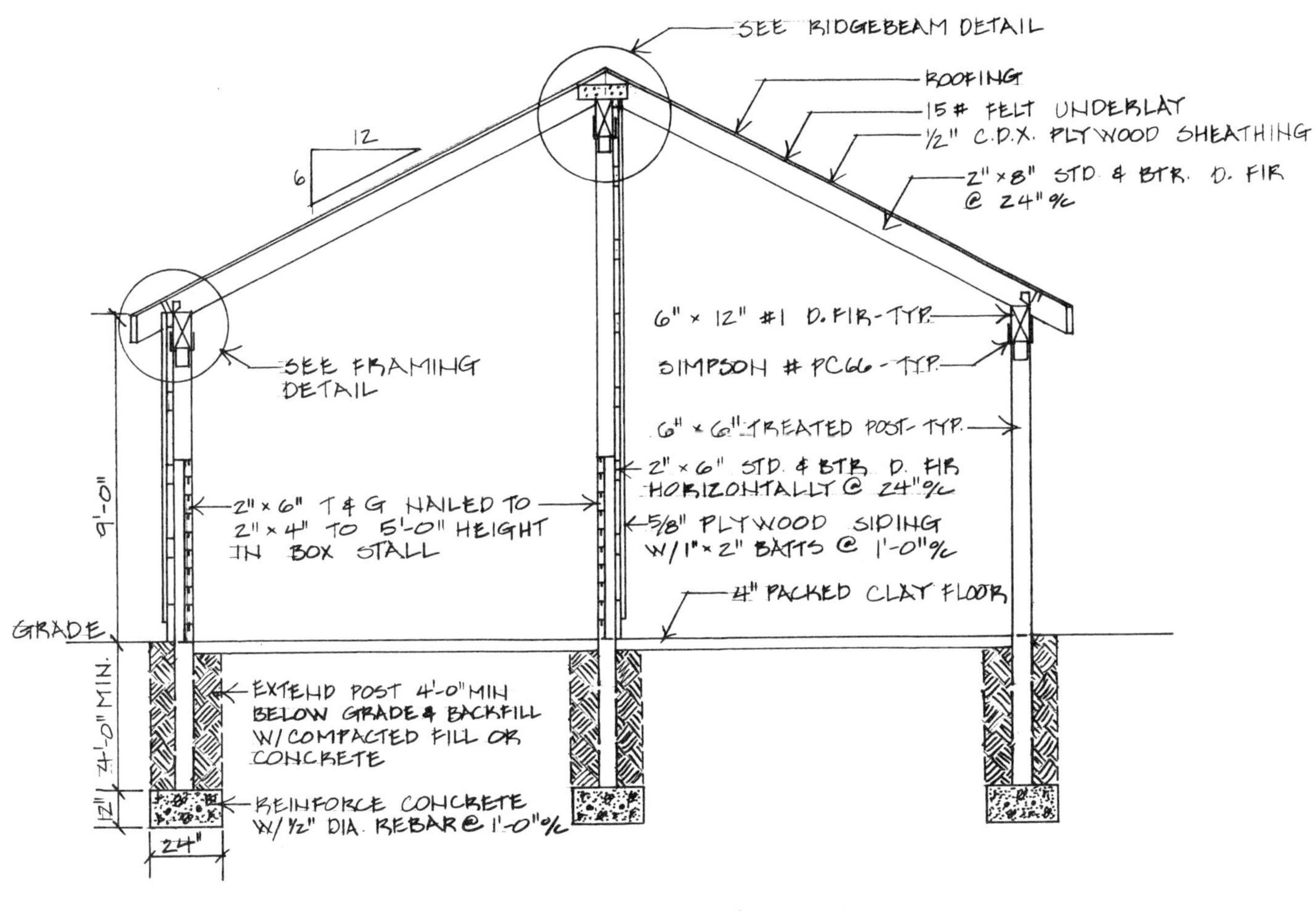


CROSS SECTION

The pole frame structure uses 6 x 6 pressure-treated posts buried 4 feet in the ground for a structural grid.

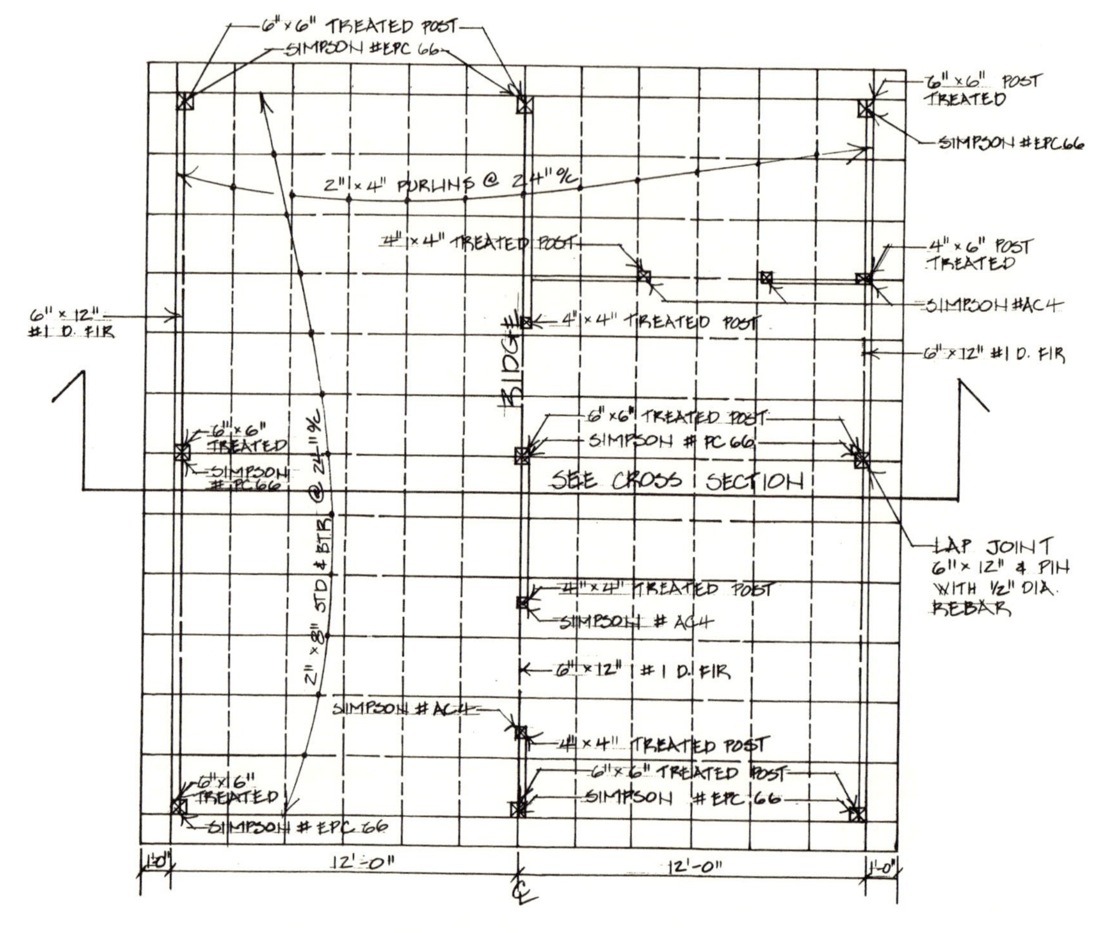


For a metal roof, 2 x 4 purlins are attached to the rafters to provide support every two feet.

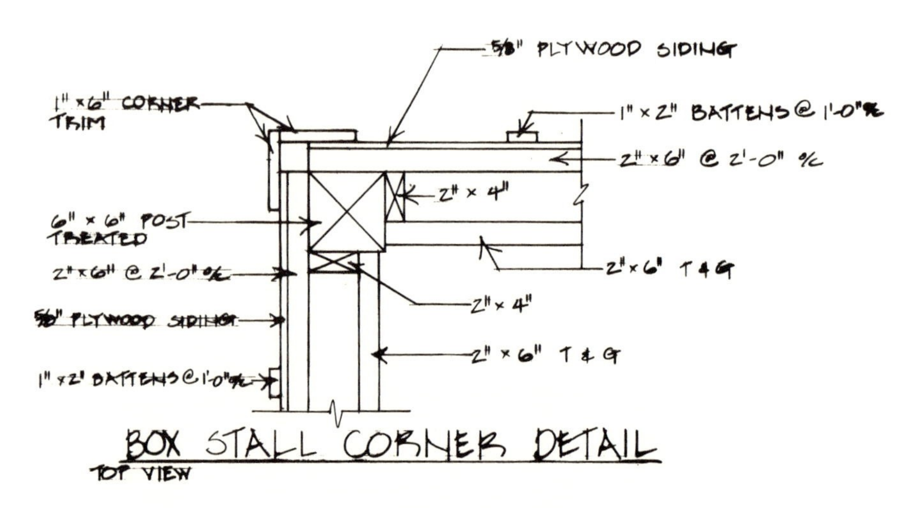


Stalls are enclosed with tongue-and-groove boards to provide a sturdy "horse-proof" wall.

## The Winchester

This practical barn has a high open ceiling above half the main level, as well as 10-foot-high doors to allow ample room for farm equipment or an R.V. A garage/shop version provides parking, plus a workshop or craft studio area. The large loft provide ample storage, and can even be extended the entire length of the barn if desired. The Winchester is 21'6" tall.

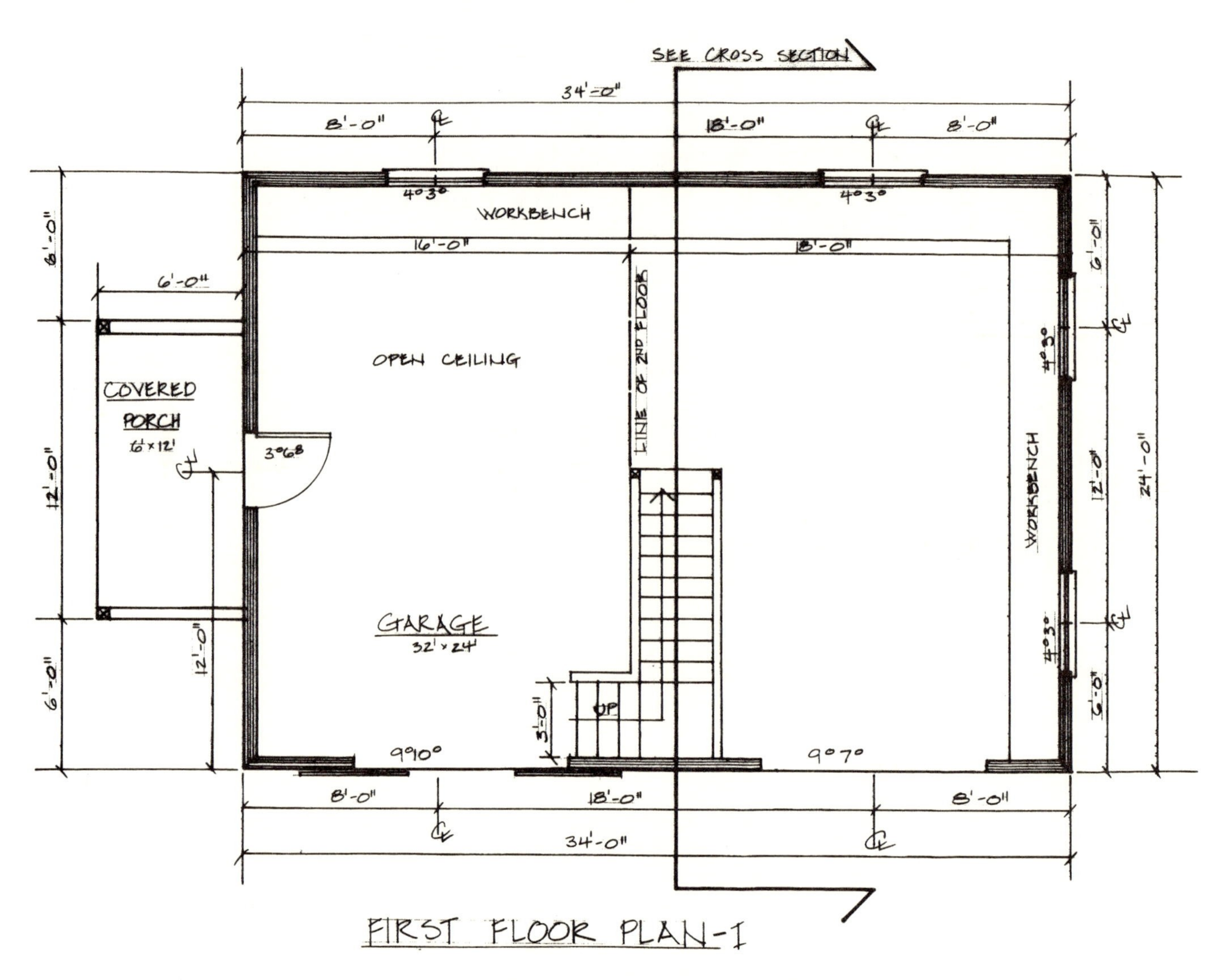


The garage/shop floor plan provides room for over 50 lineal feet of workspace.

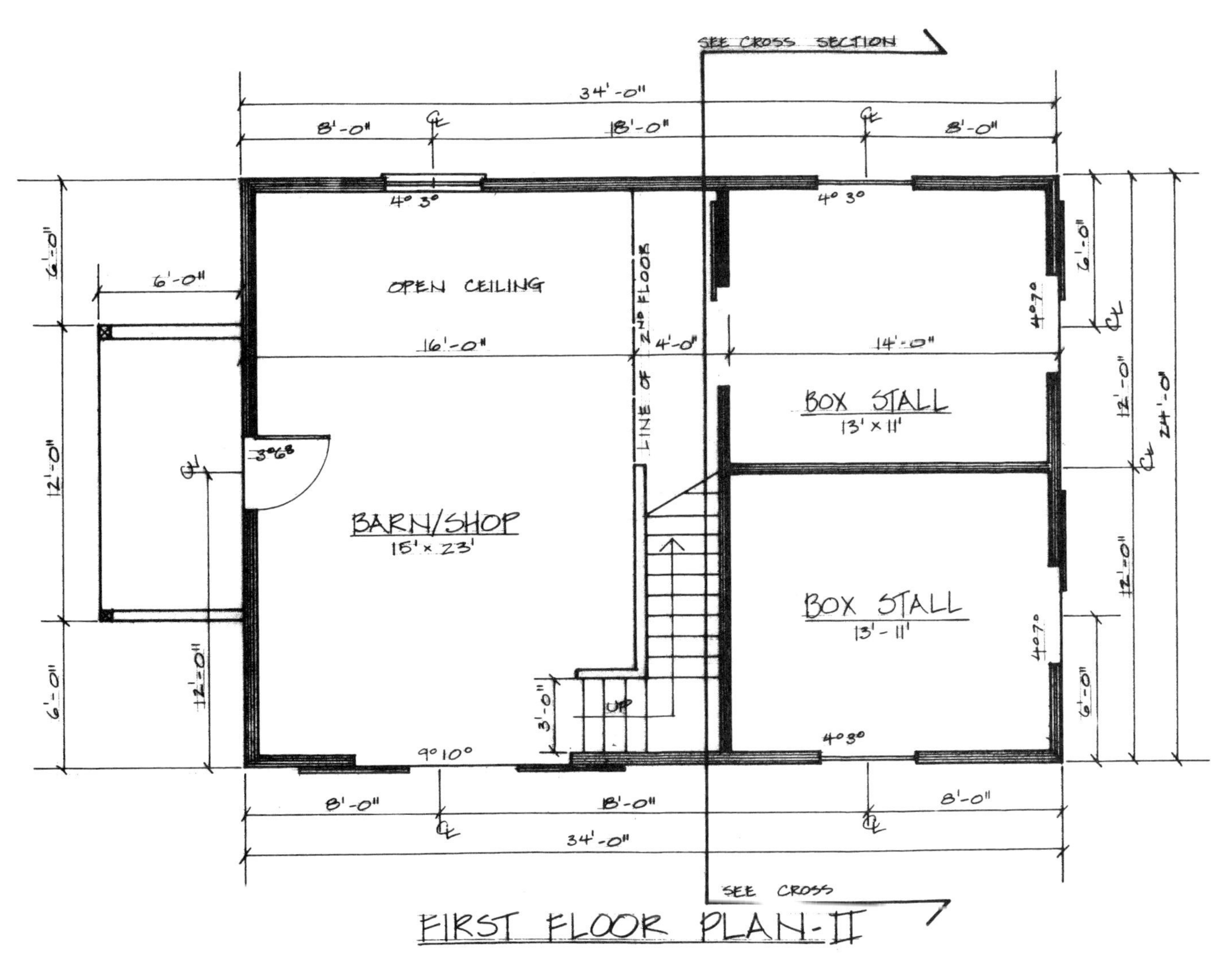


FIRST FLOOR PLAN-II

The barn/stable plan has two generous stalls and a high-ceilinged area for tall equipment.

The old-fashioned barn doors can be built on site,
or manufactured overhead doors can be substituted.

A compact porch provides a sheltered spot for a rocker or two.

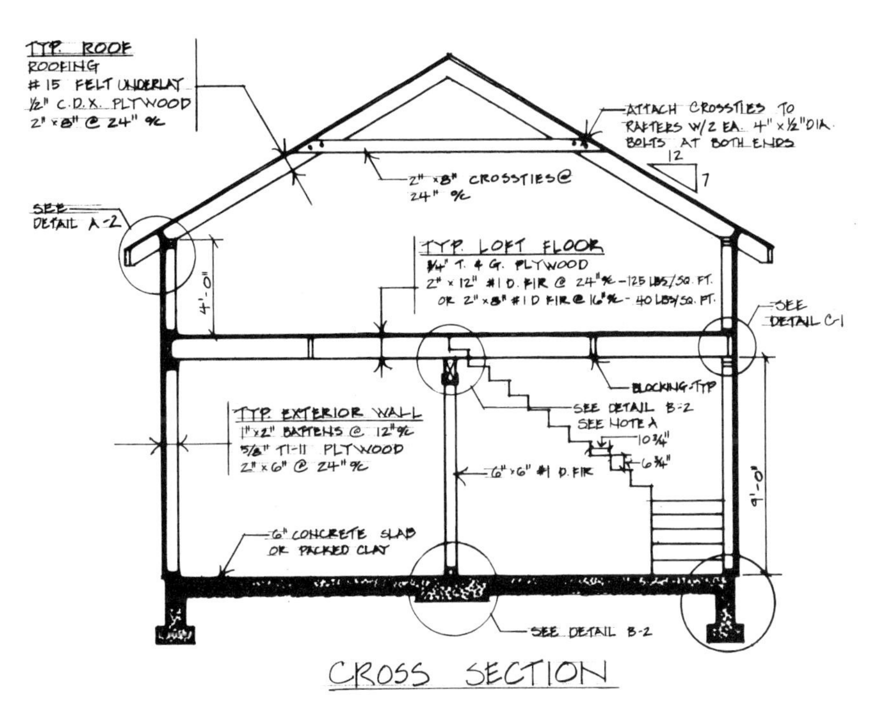


The loft floor can be built to handle either light loads or heavy loads, such as hay.

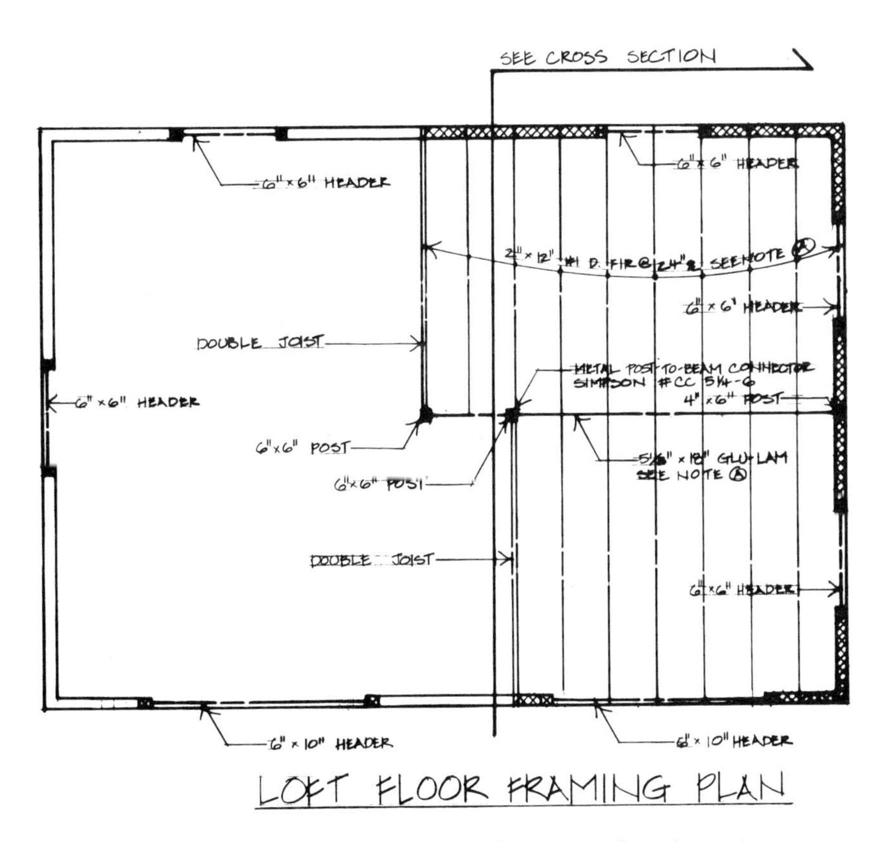


Simply duplicating the loft floor framing on the other side of the stairwell creates a full loft.

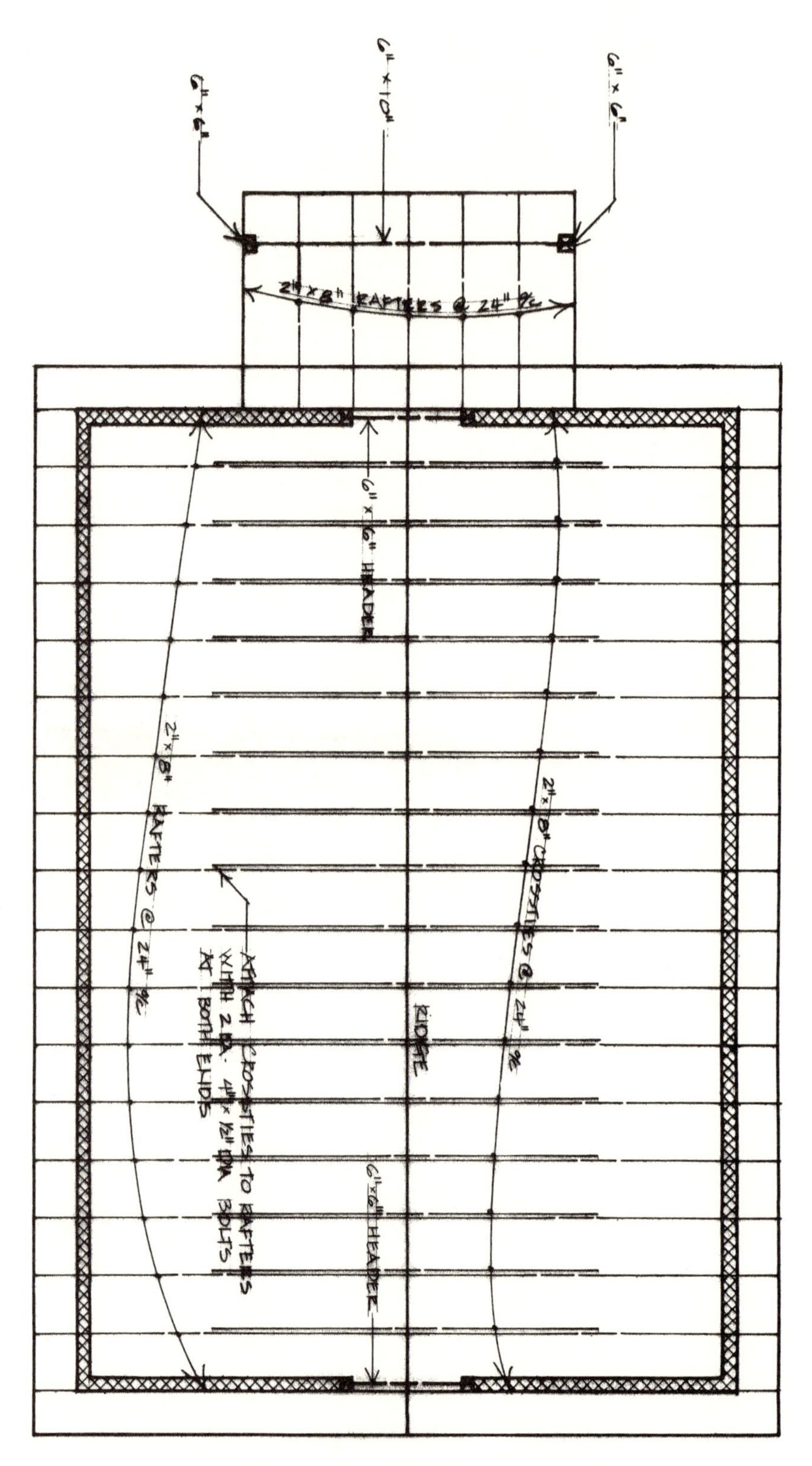


ROOF FRAMING PLAN

A ridge beam could be substituted for cross-ties to provide a cathedral-ceiling loft.

# The Cascade

The Cascade can be built as a working barn with a large storage loft, as a single-car garage with a greenhouse wing, or as a workshop/studio for the craftsperson. A "barnhouse" version has been a popular compact home. The simple shape and compact size of the Cascade help keep construction costs low. Overall height is 23'.

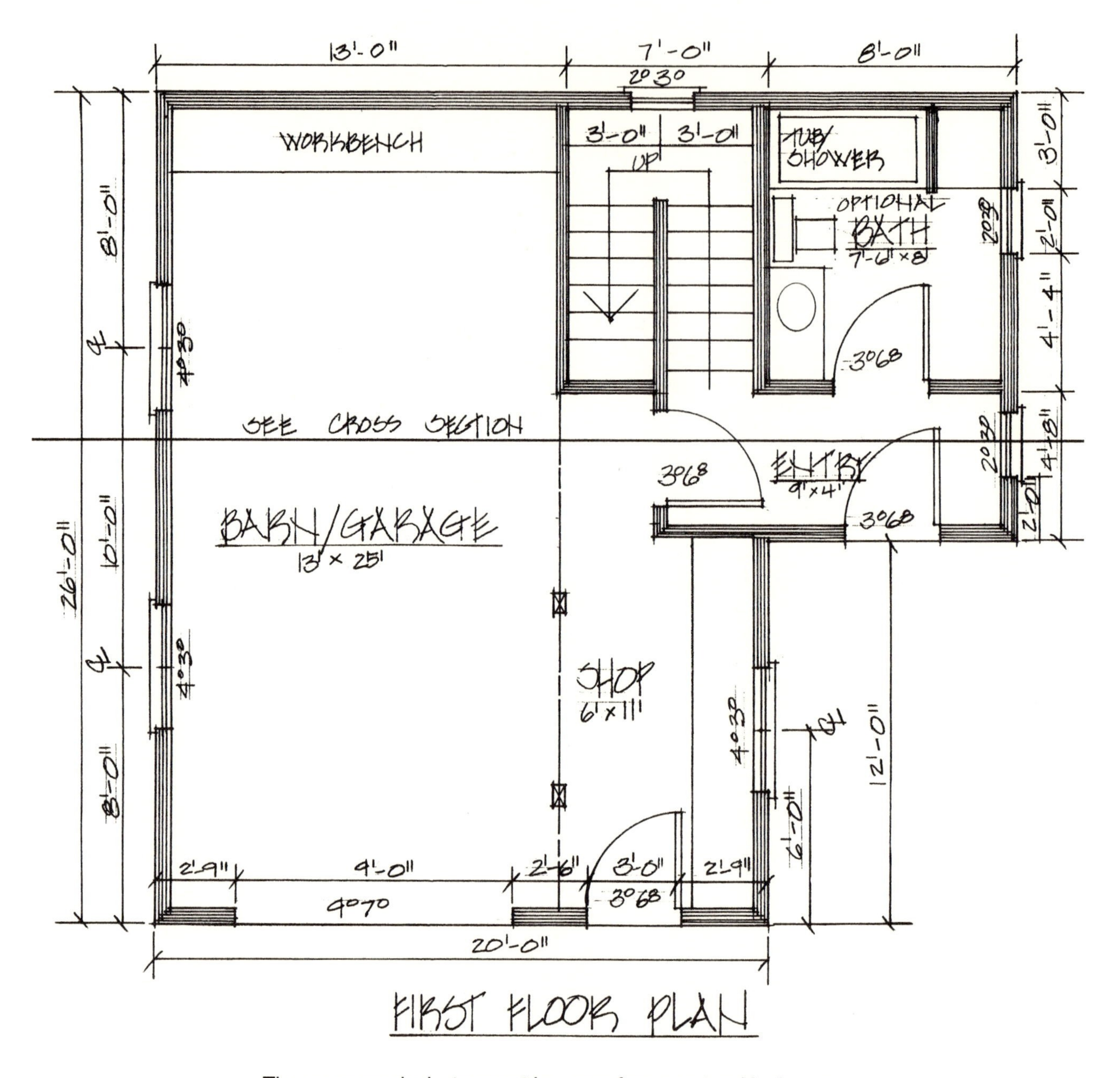


The one story shed wing provides room for an optional bathroom or a sunny greenhouse for the gardener.

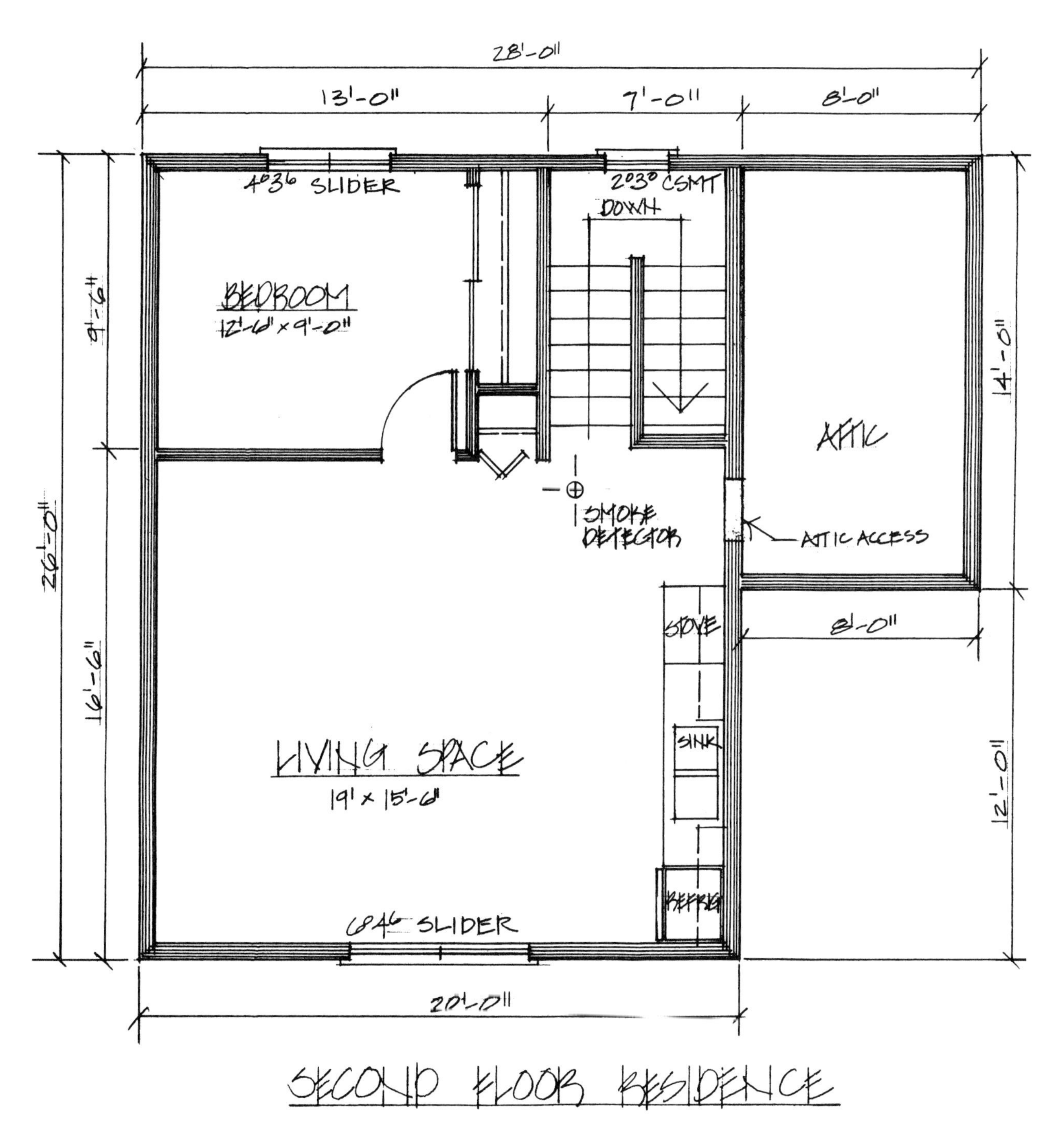


Interior stairs lead to a well lit loft area that can be used as an apartment, an artist's studio, or just for storage.

An extra entry door allows the separation of the lower level from the loft.

Economical plywood sheathing/siding contributes to the affordability of the Cascade plan.

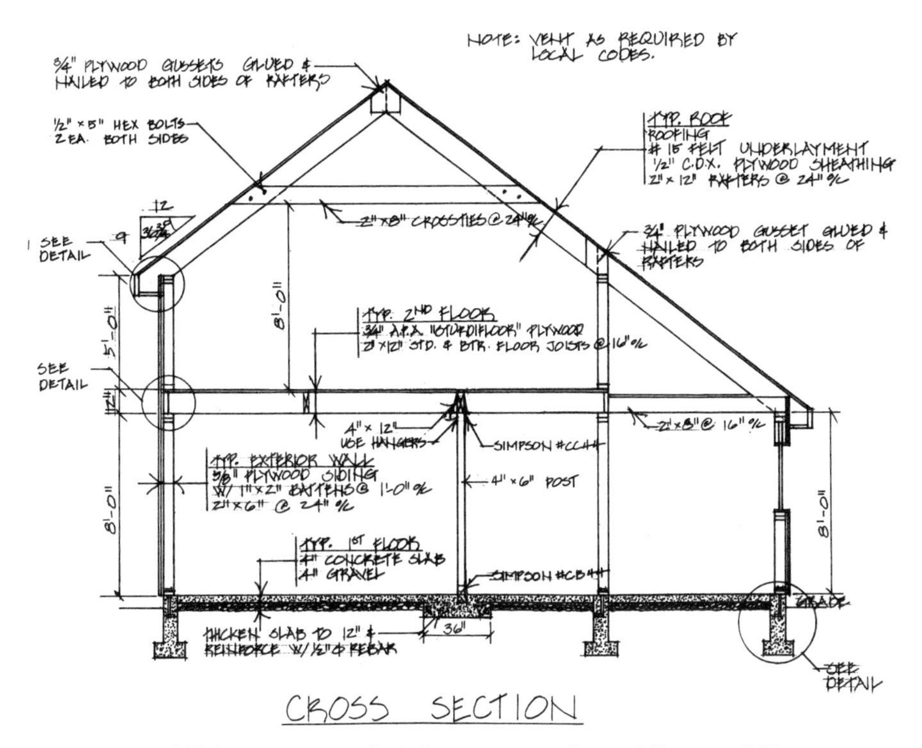


With a perimeter foundation, a joisted wood floor could be substituted for the concrete slab. 12-inch rafters allow ample room for insulation and venting if the interior is heated.

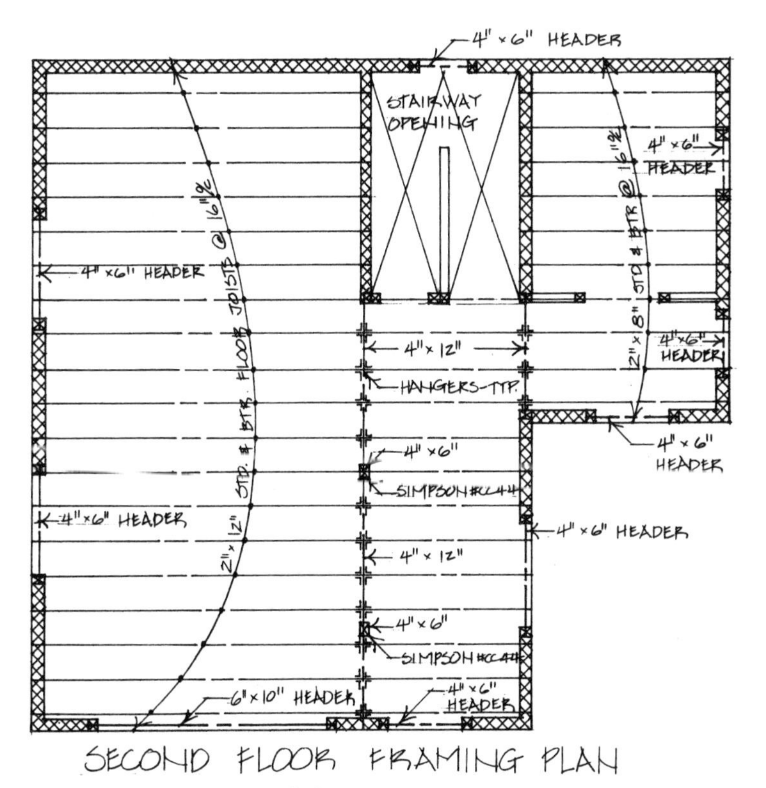


A sturdy loft floor can handle heavy loads.

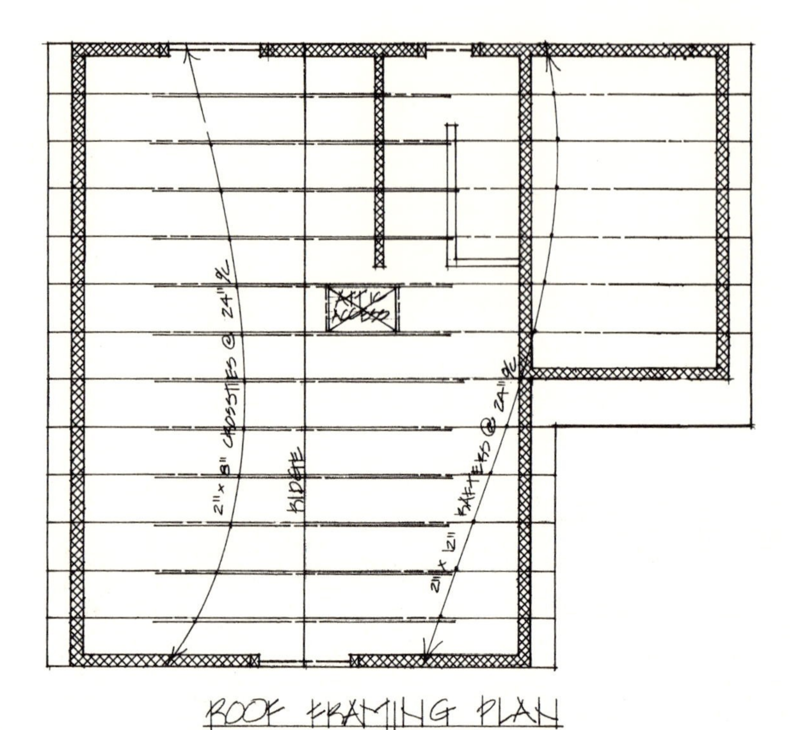


Simple roof framing is quick and easy to build.

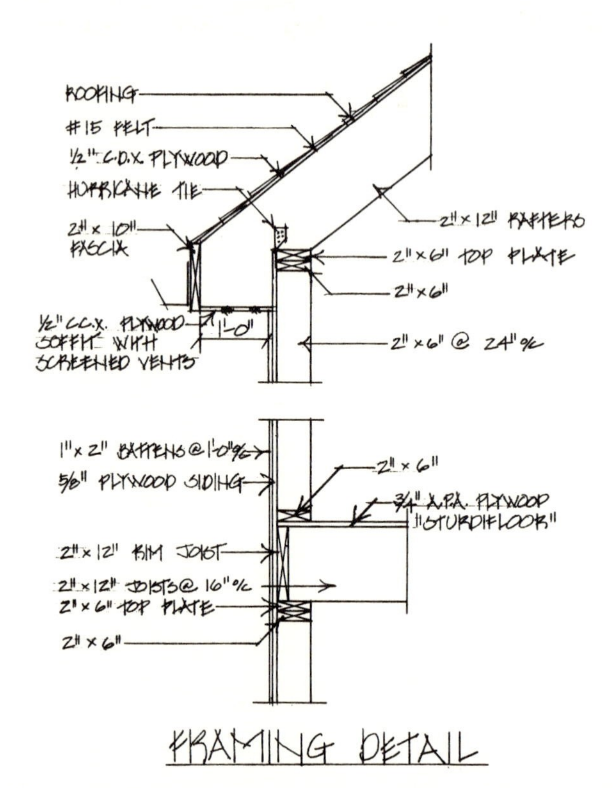


Plywood siding spans the rim joist, tying both floors together.
The hurricane ties attach the roof to the walls.

# The Monterey

This large barn/stable has six large stalls and separate rooms for feed and tack. Large sliding doors at each end of the center alley, and Dutch outside doors for each stall, help ventilate the barn in warm weather. The loft runs the full length of the barn above the alley, providing ample storage. The Monterey is 19' tall.

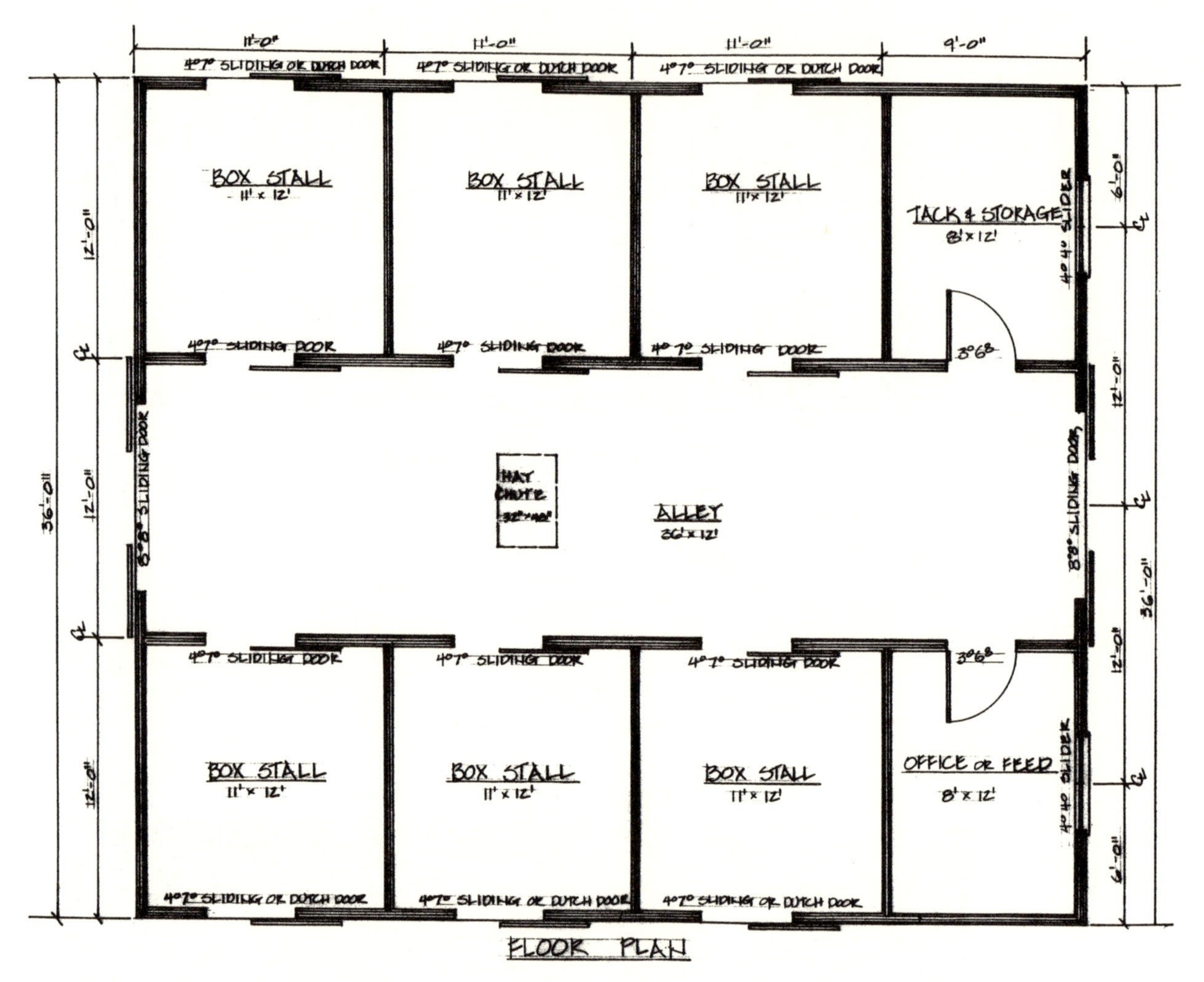


Although a centrally located loft access is shown, hay can be placed in each stall directly from the hayloft for convenience.

FRONT ELEVATION

Convenient loading doors at both ends of the loft allow easy access.
Large windows in the feed and tack rooms
provide natural light and ventilation.

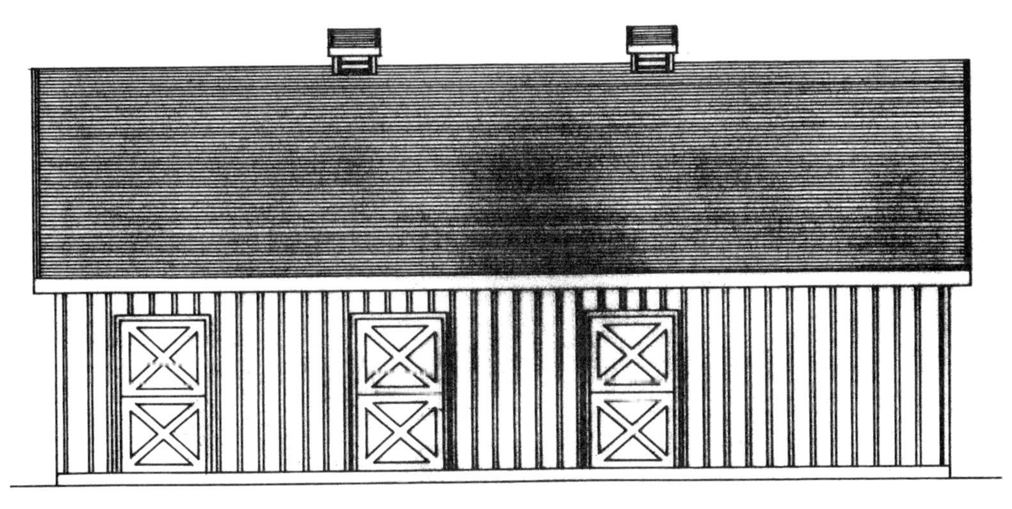

SIDE ELEVATION

Each stall has both an inside and outside door.

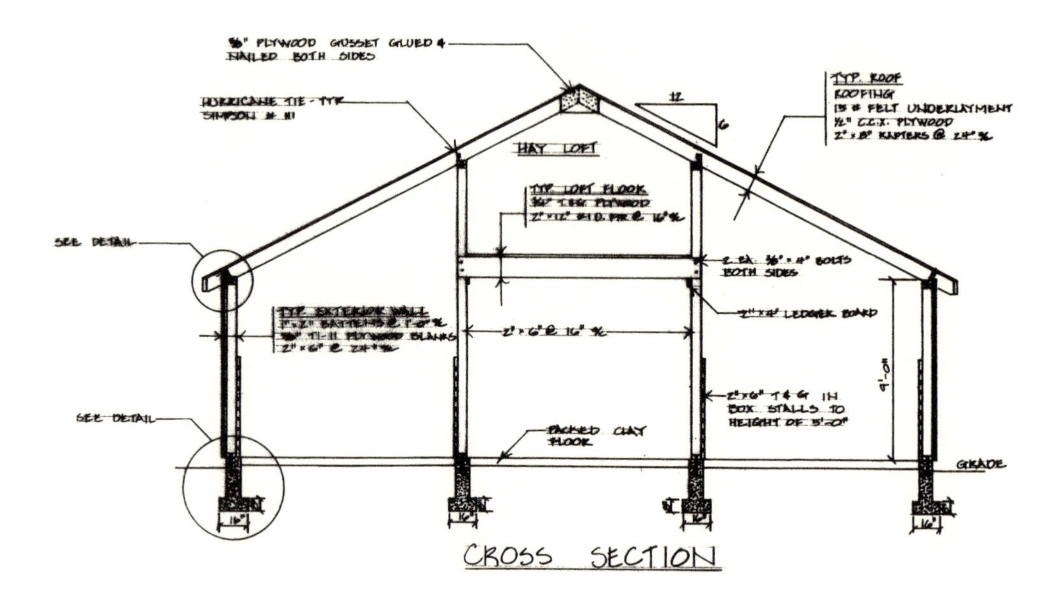

Using rafters instead of manufactured trusses allows room for a spacious hayloft.

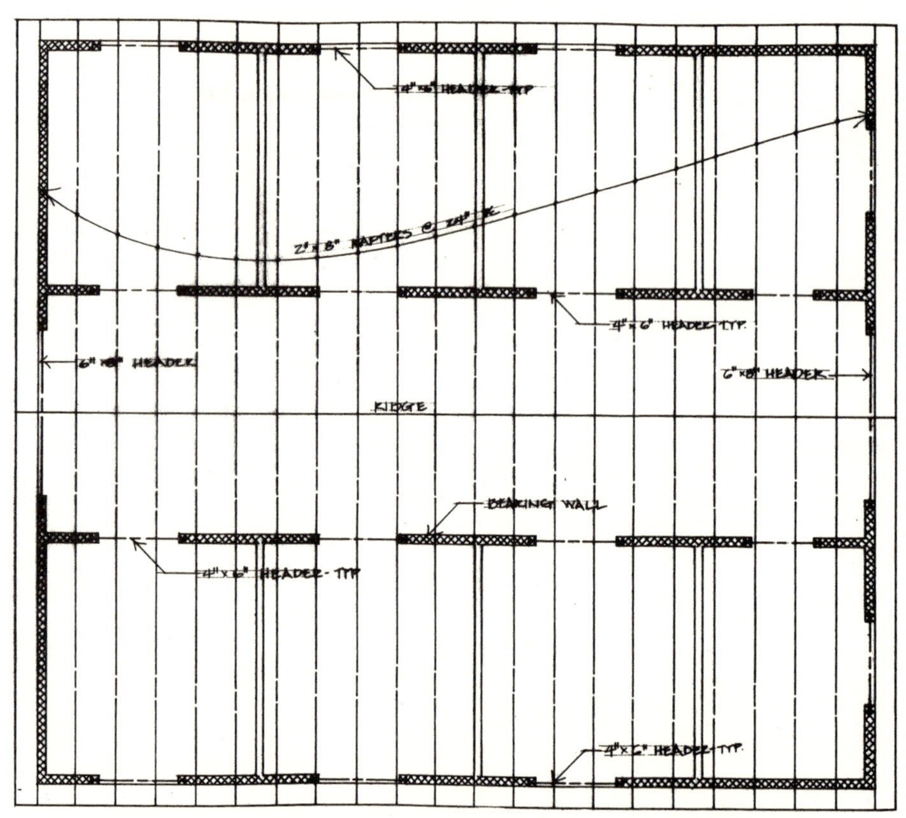

Because the stall partitions are non-structural, they can be adjusted to fit large or small animals, or to combine two stalls to form a foaling stall.

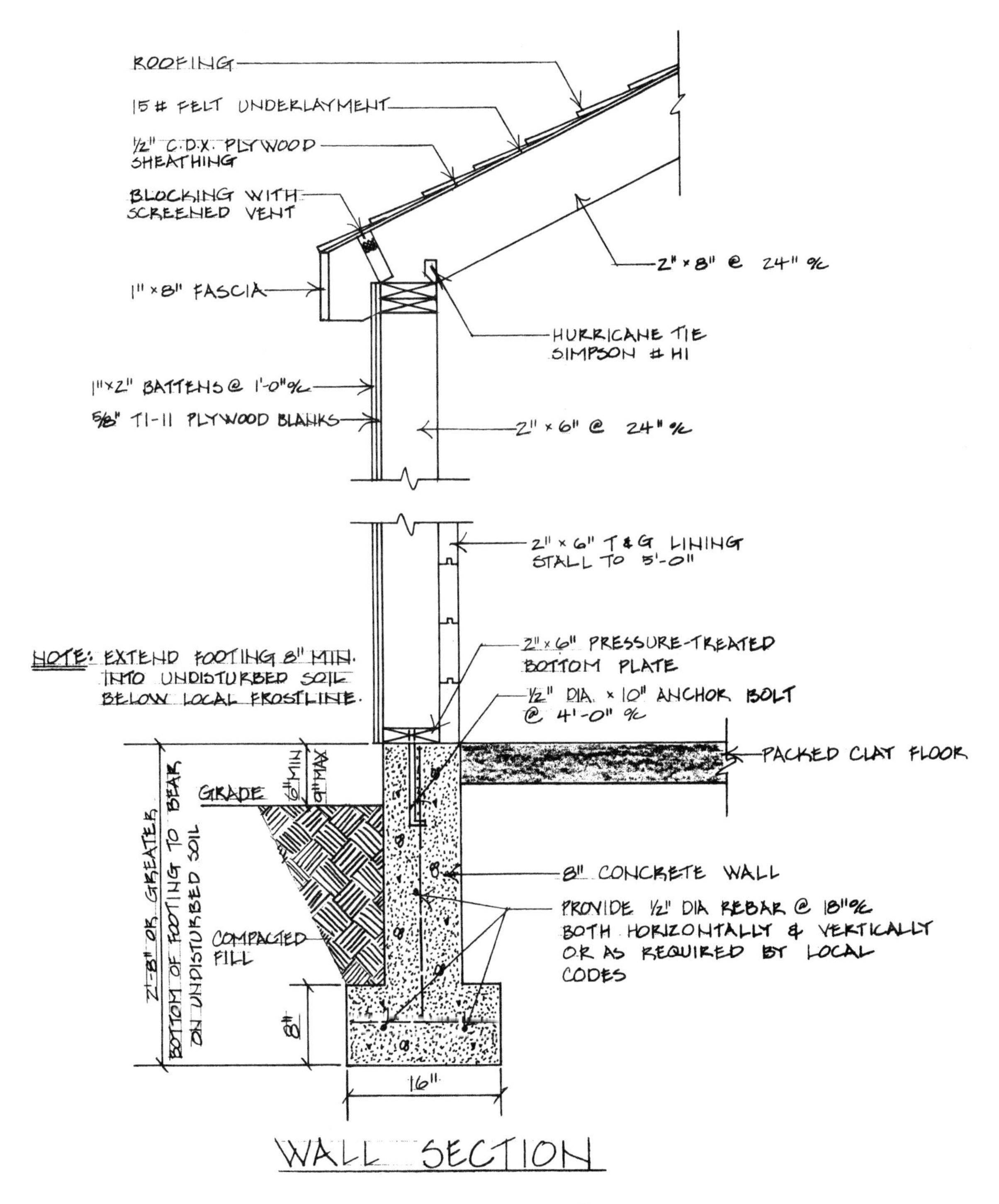


A concrete foundation will last several lifetimes, and improves resale value.

J.R. SMITH

# Gambrel Roof Barn Plans

## The Yaquina

The Yaquina is the smallest in our series of traditional gambrel barns. It's just the right size for a smaller collection of animals, or a workshop or an artist's studio. With living space on the ground floor, and sleeping space in the large loft, the Yaquina makes a fine mini-barn house. The height is 19' 6".

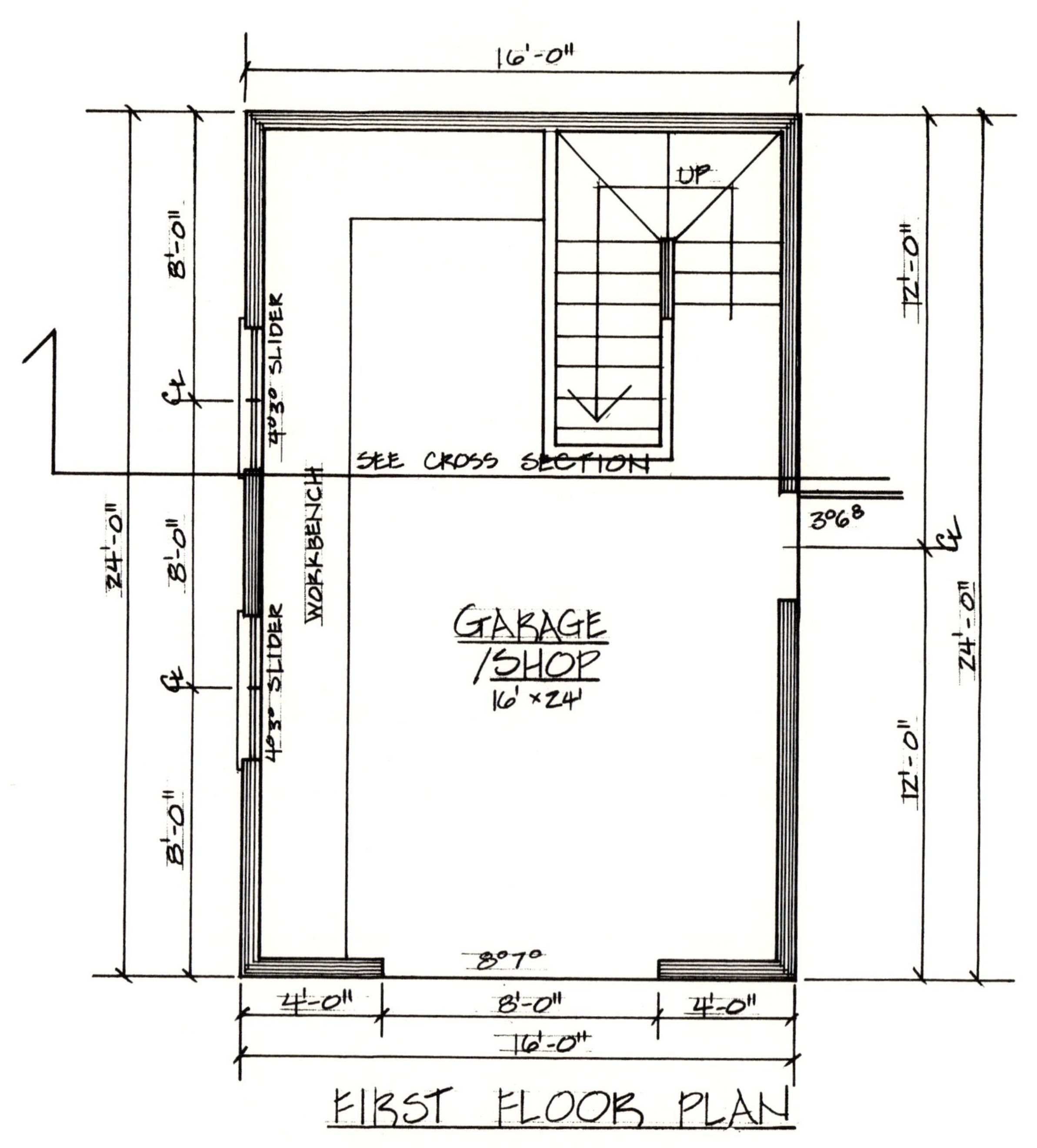


Substituting a "pull-down" attic stair for the full-size stairwell provides more space for vehicles on the ground floor.

The main access door can be a hinged swinging door, a sliding door on an overhead track, or an overhead garage door with an electric opener.

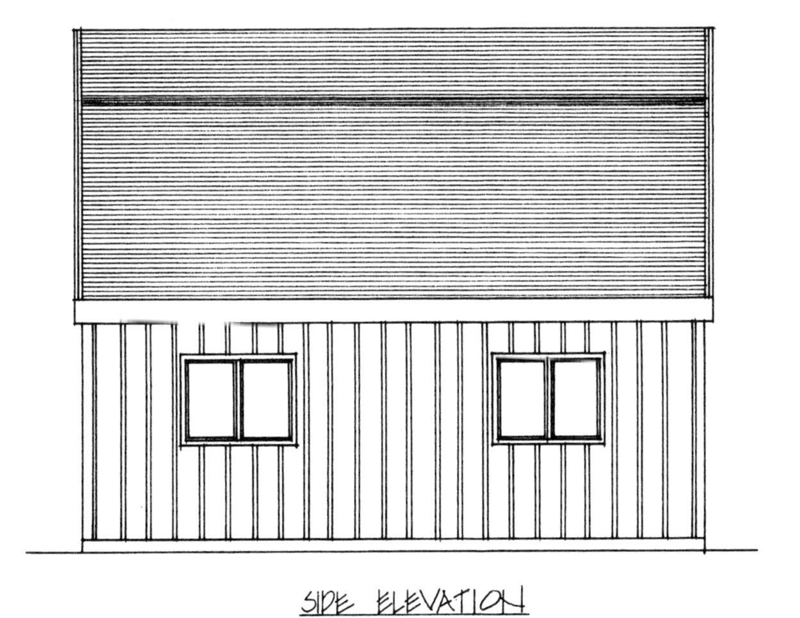


The sliding windows provide light to the workbench area, and ventilation when needed.

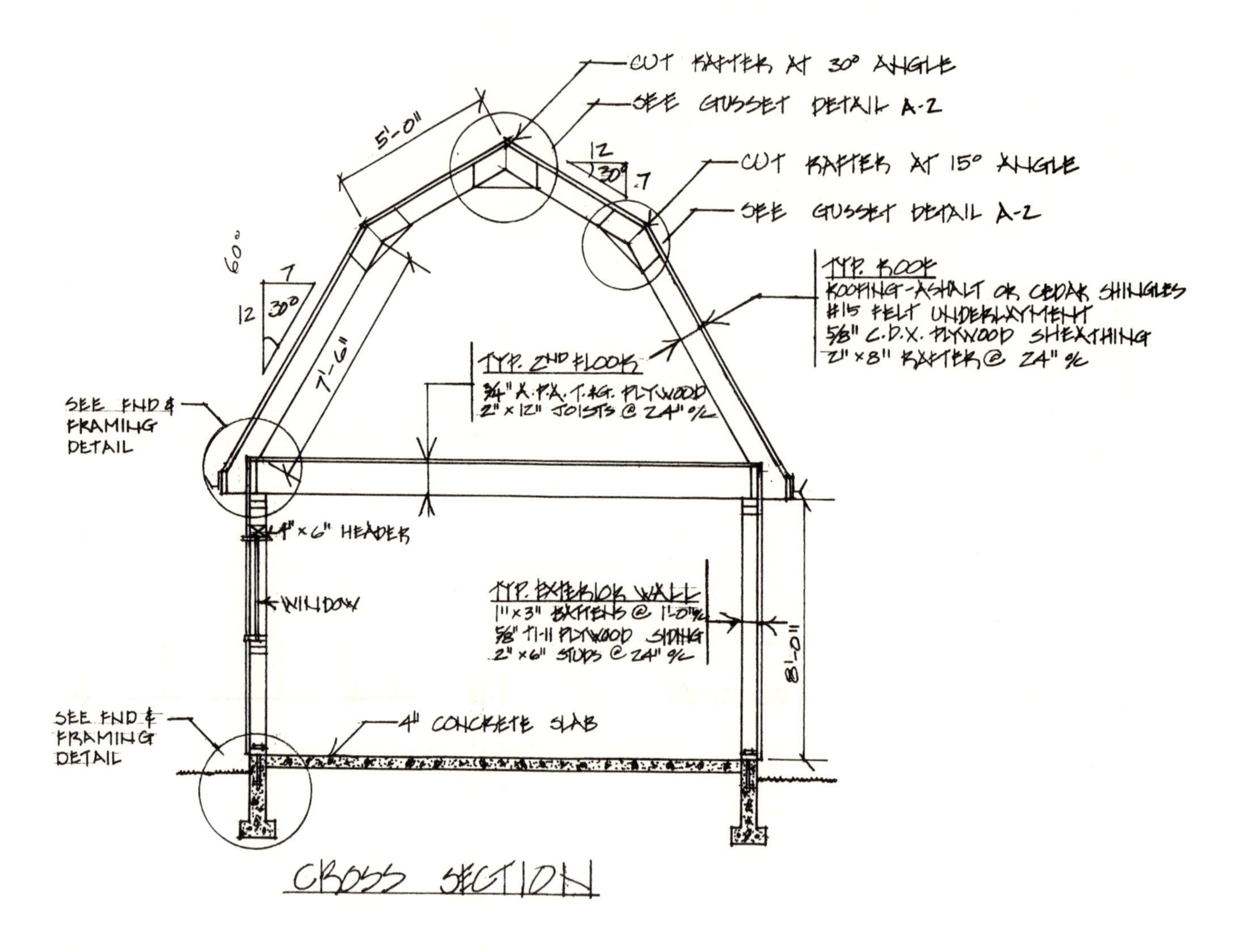


The gambrel roof shape provides more usable space in the loft, and clear-span trusses eliminate interior posts.

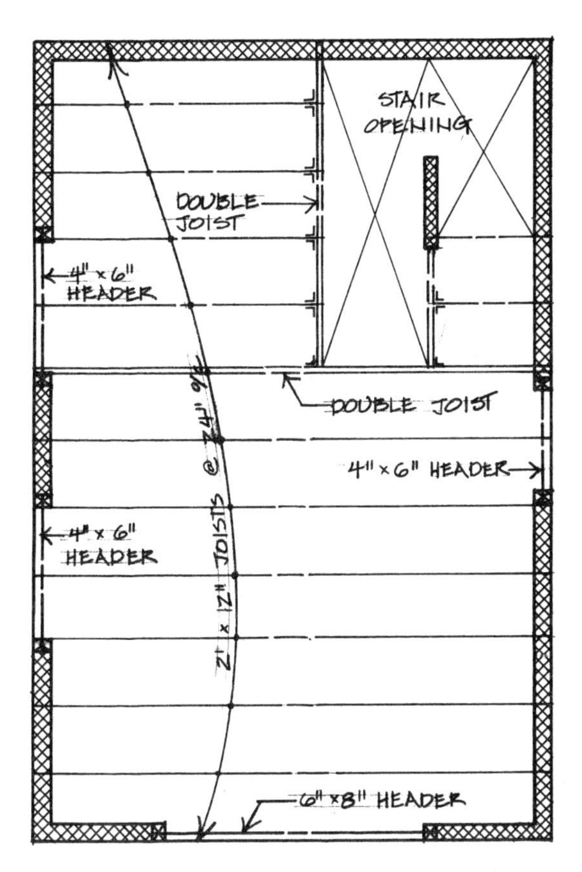


LOFT FLOOR FRAMING PLAN

The 12-inch joists span the width of the Yaquina without interior posts or beams. For heavy loft loads, the joist spacing could be changed to 12 or 16 inches on center.

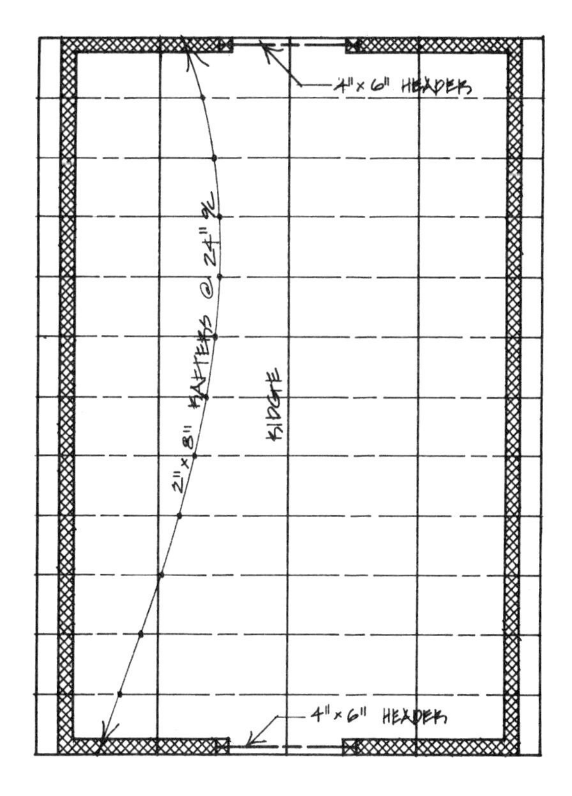


ROOF FRAMING PLAN

A manufactured "storage truss" can be substituted for the site-built truss.

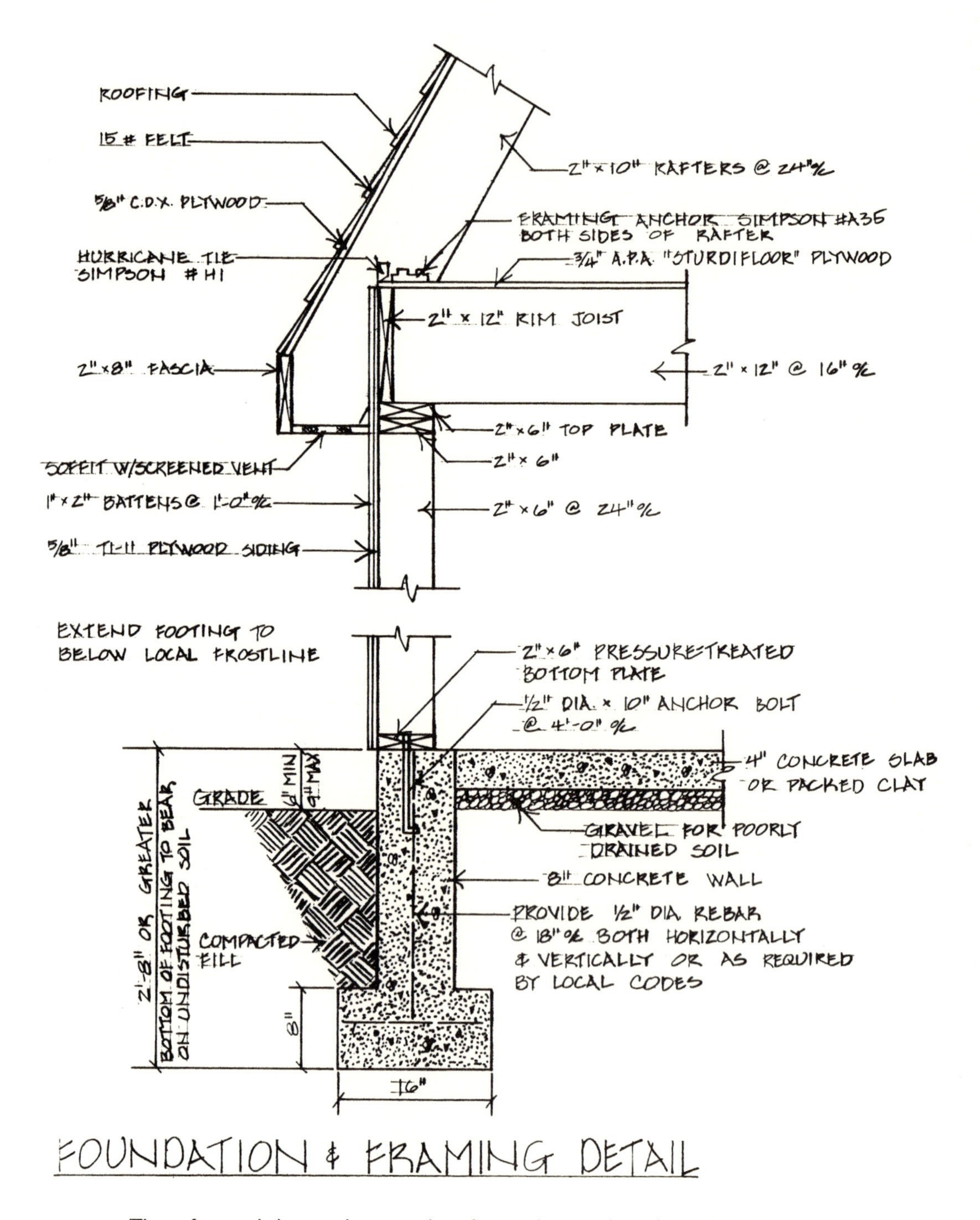


The rafter ends have a deep notch to lower the visual roofline of the Yaquina.

# The Tillamook

The Tillamook is a practical gambrel barn design. It can be built as a barn, with animals on the ground floor and a large hayloft/storage above, or as a two-car garage/shop. The height is 21' 6".

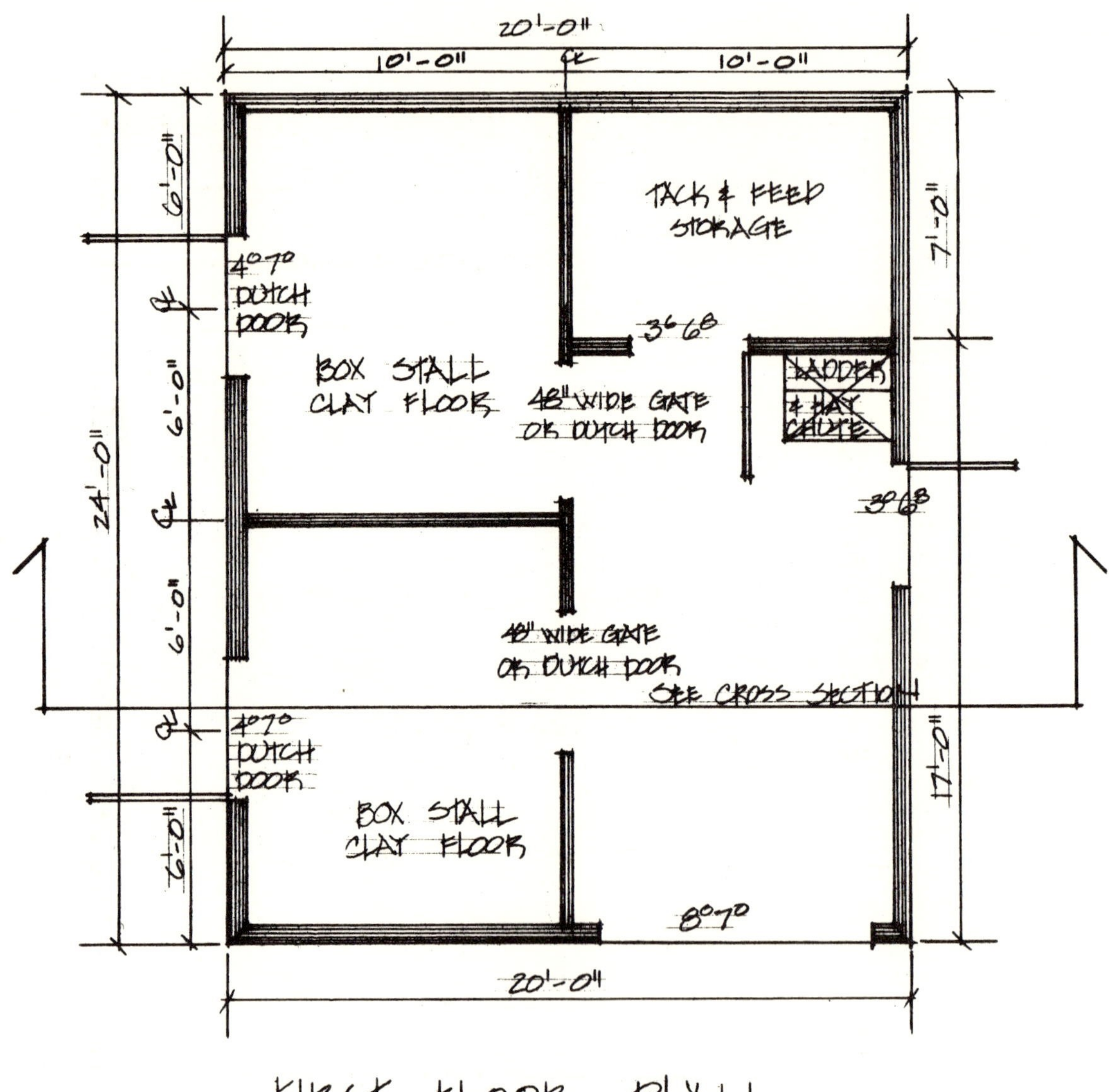


# FIRST FLOOR PLAN

Two 10 x 12 box stalls include both interior and exterior doors for easy access. A storage room provides ample space for the needs of two horses. To save space, a built-in ladder provides access to the hayloft.

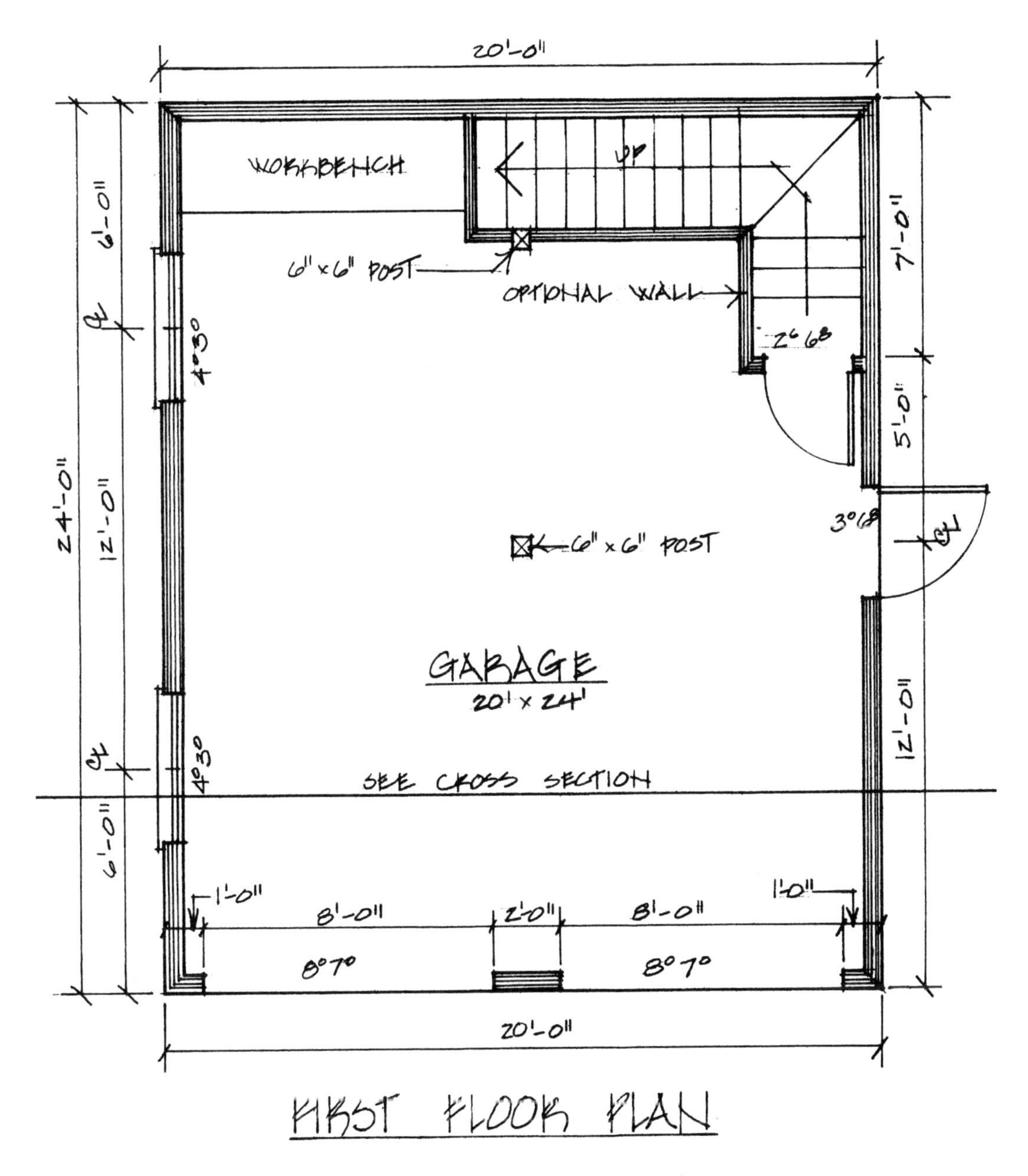


The garage floor plan for the Tillamook includes a full staircase
to access the loft area. The center post and beam can be eliminated,
if necessary, by using manufactured floor joists to clear-span the width of the building.

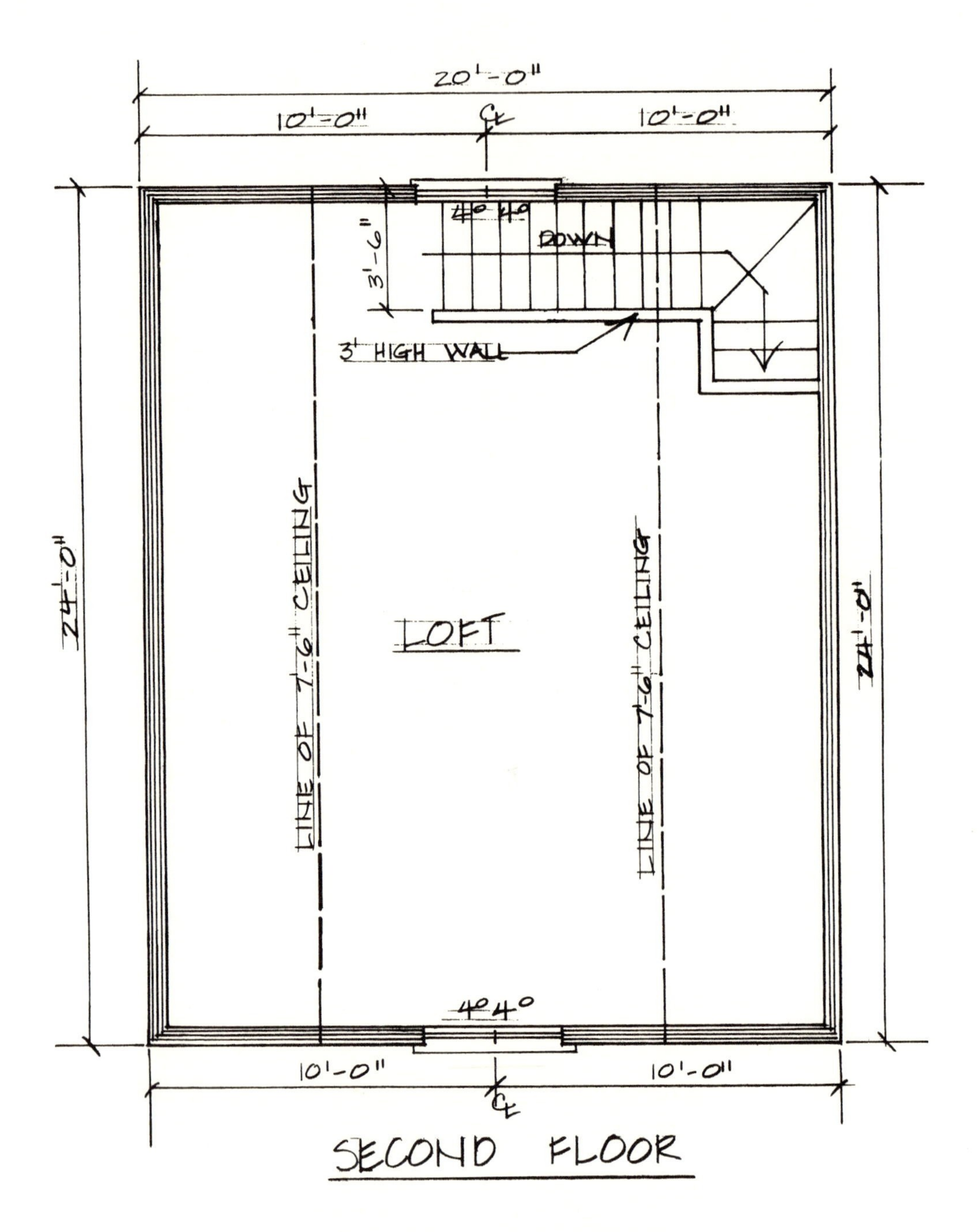


The generous loft can be used for storage, a studio, or even as a sleeping area for a compact "barn house".

This front elevation for the garage version of the Tillamook shows separate doors, although a single 16-foot overhead door could be substituted.

The side elevation for the Tillamook garage plan shows sliding windows. In the barn version, Dutch doors may be substituted.

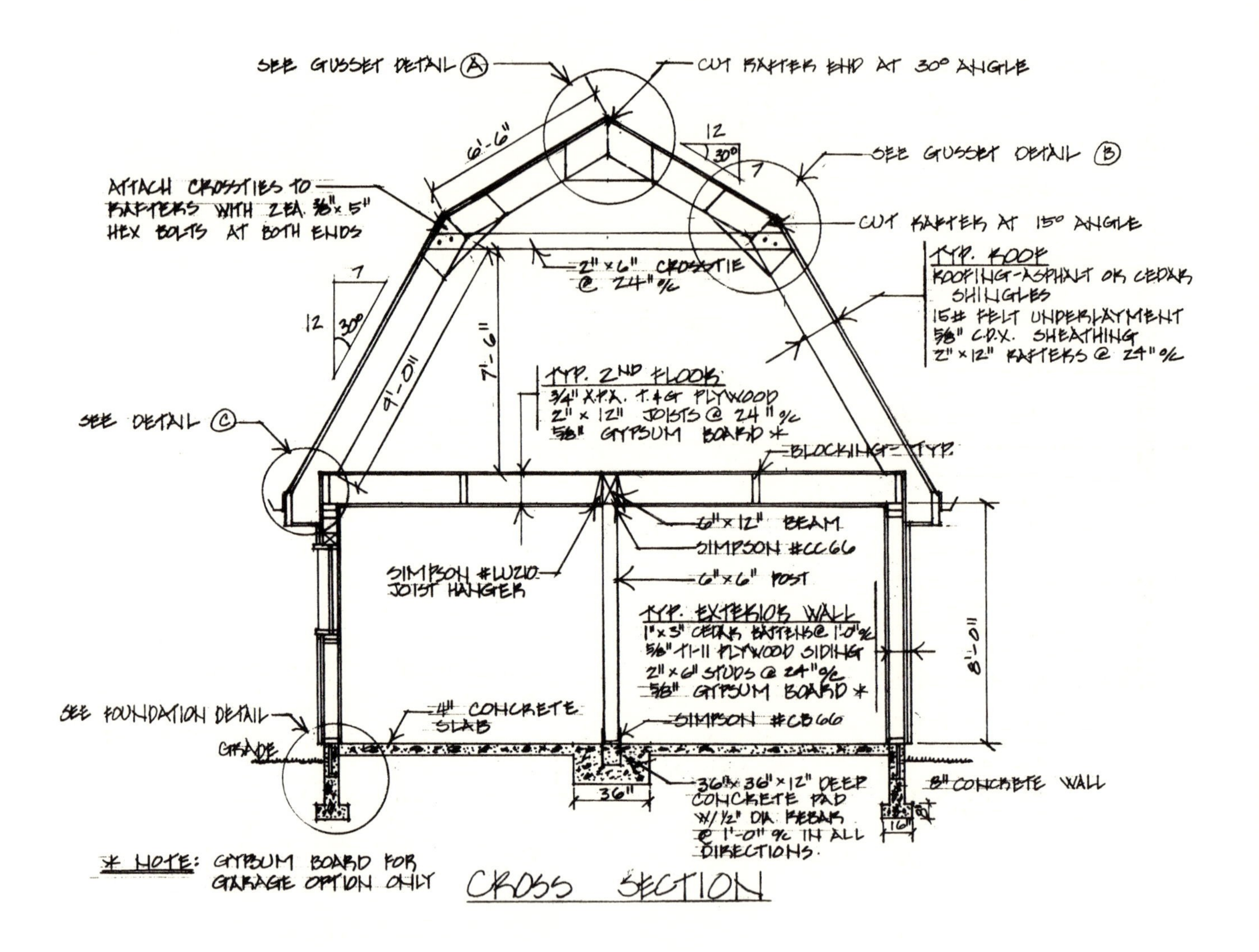


An optional cross-tie provides the framing for a flat ceiling in the loft area. Manufactured gambrel trusses can also be substituted for the site-built trusses, but with a loss of loft space.

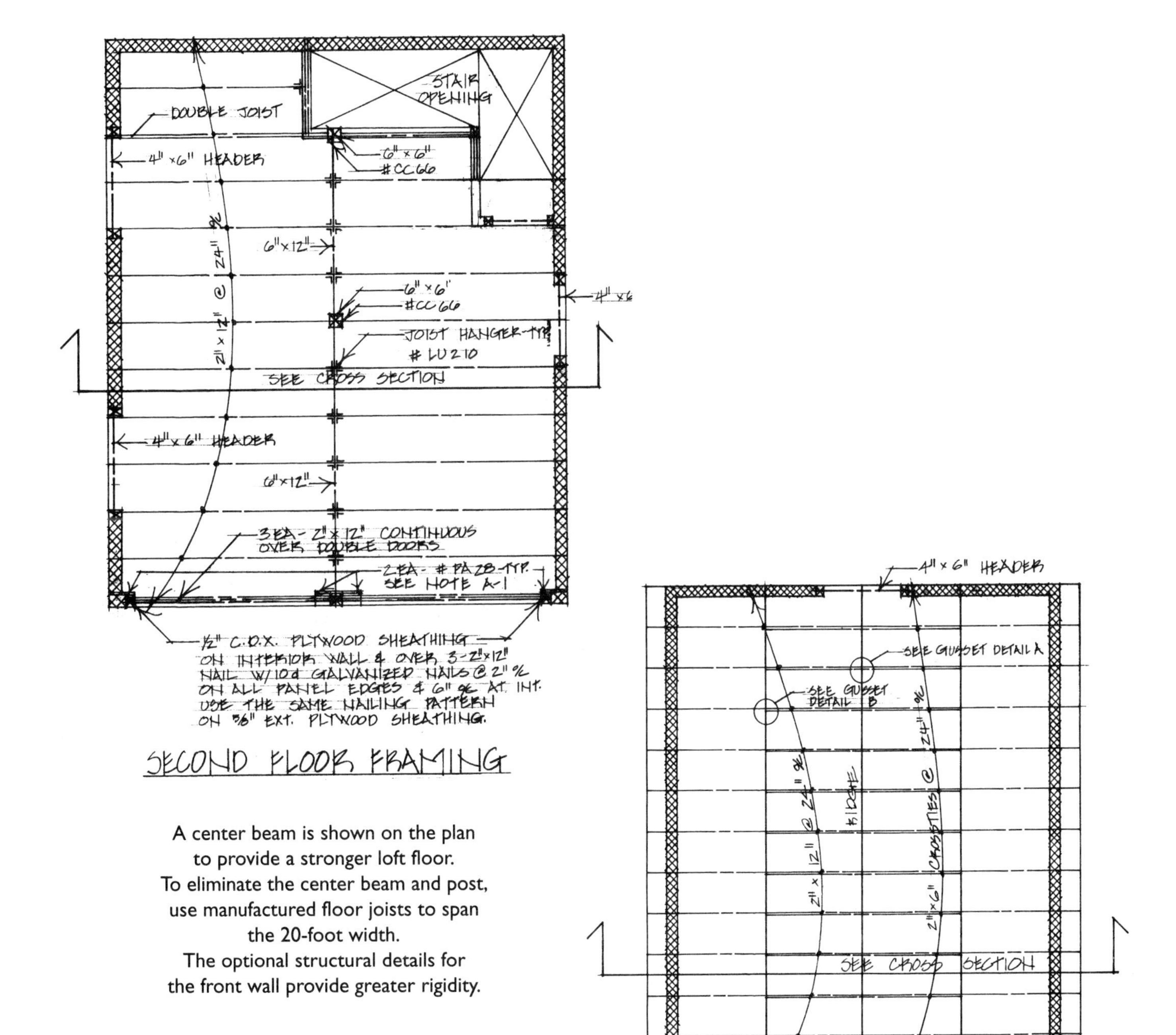


A center beam is shown on the plan
to provide a stronger loft floor.
To eliminate the center beam and post,
use manufactured floor joists to span
the 20-foot width.
The optional structural details for
the front wall provide greater rigidity.

The 2 x 12 rafters provide extra room
for insulation when a
heated space is required.

## The Cambridge

The Cambridge gambrel barn provides room for up to three stalls.
It can also be used as a garage or workshop. The full loft doubles the usable space, and has more than 8 feet of headroom.
The Cambridge is 24' 6" tall.

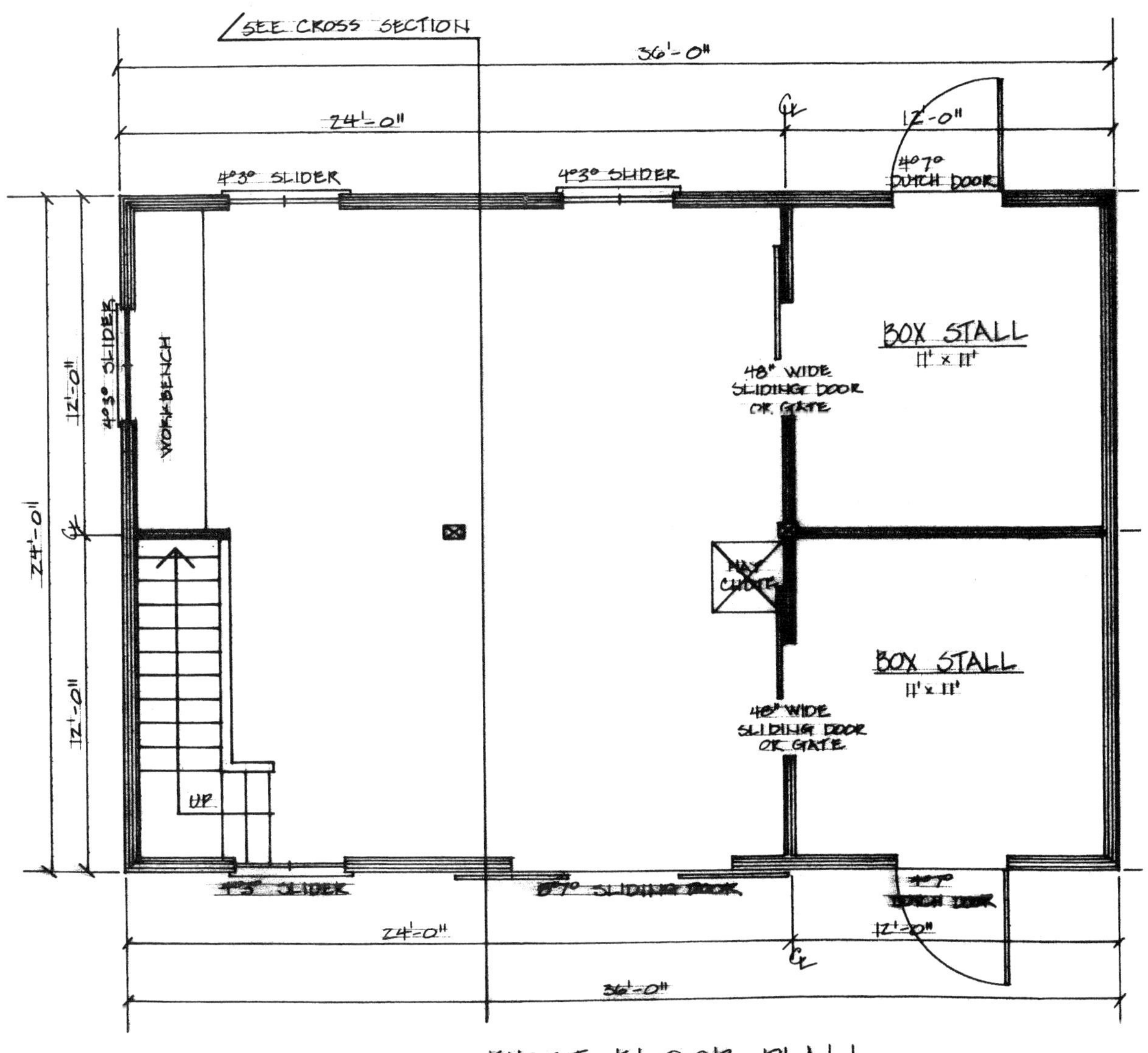


FIRST FLOOR PLAN

This floor plan provides two generous stalls and room for a shop area. Both box stalls have inside and outside doors for convenience and improved ventilation.

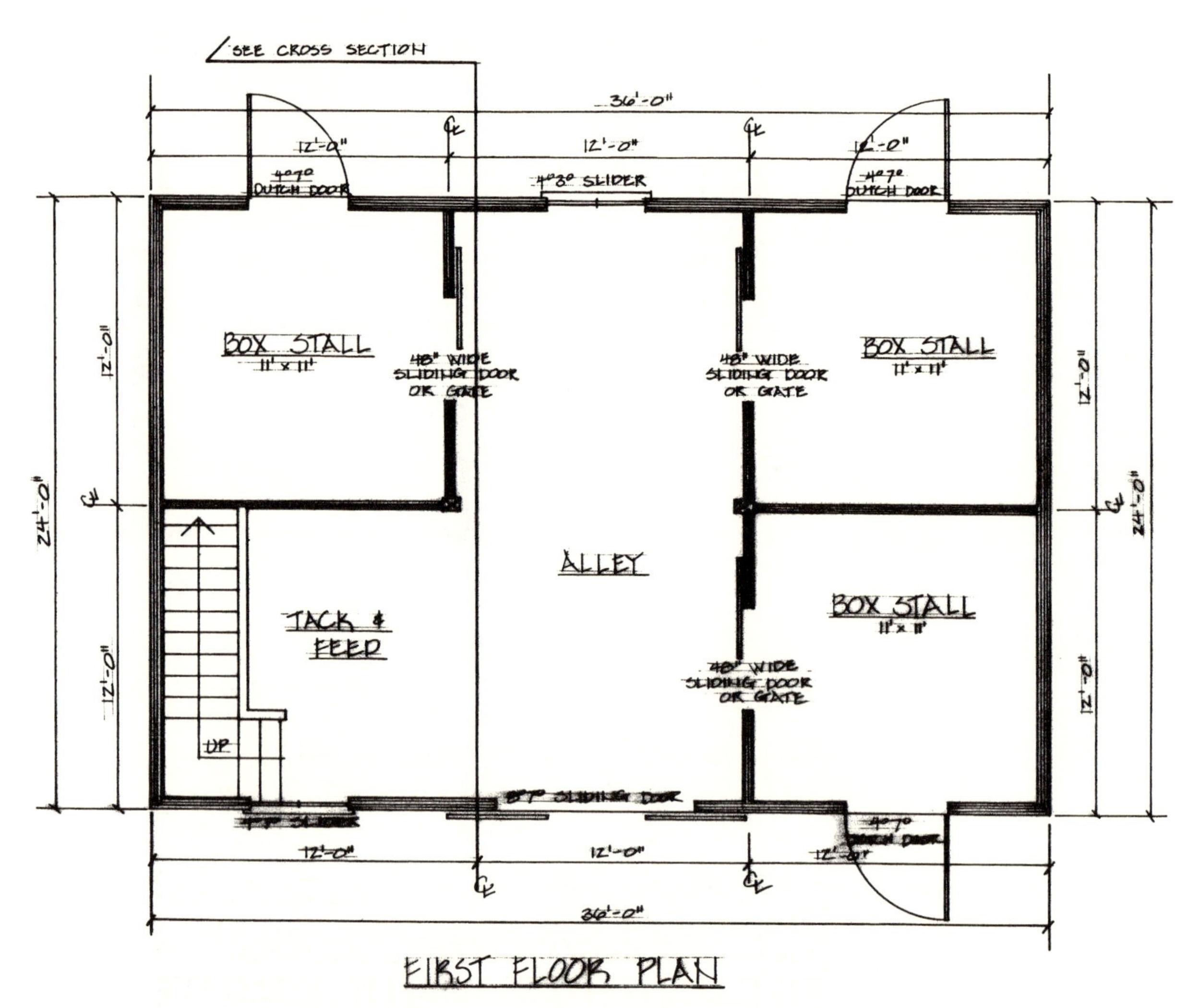


This alternate floor plan includes three box stalls and a tack and feed area that can be enclosed, if desired. A second 8-foot sliding door can be added at the other end of the alley, if needed.

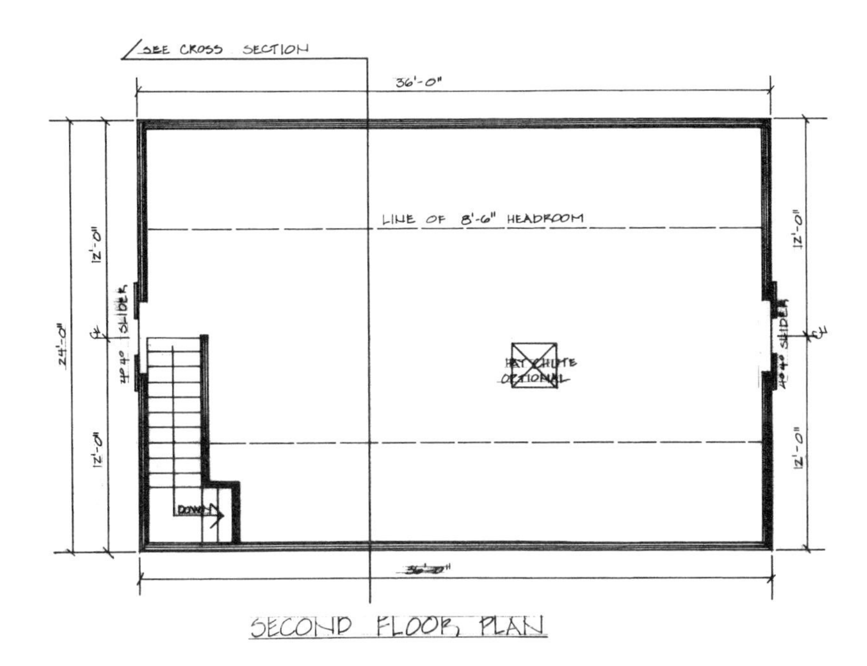


The full loft has more than 800 square feet of usable space.

An 8-foot door provides access to the center alley, and a 4-foot Dutch door to each stall.

SIDE ELEVATION

A double door at each end of the loft provides access for loading hay. Windows can be substituted, if desired.

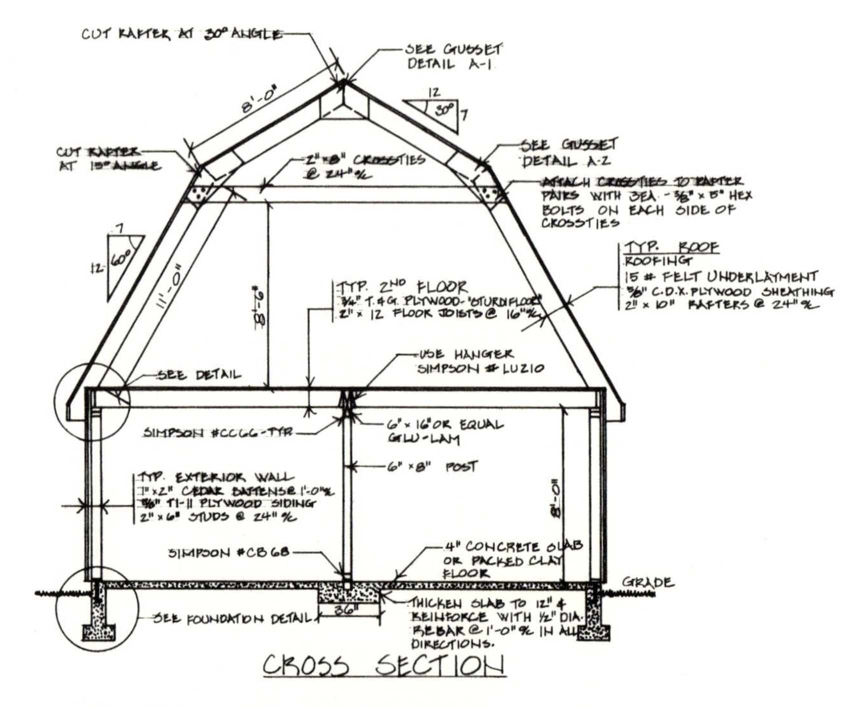


The 24-foot width of the Cambridge barn provides additional usable space in the loft area. Cross-ties allow a flat finished ceiling to be installed.

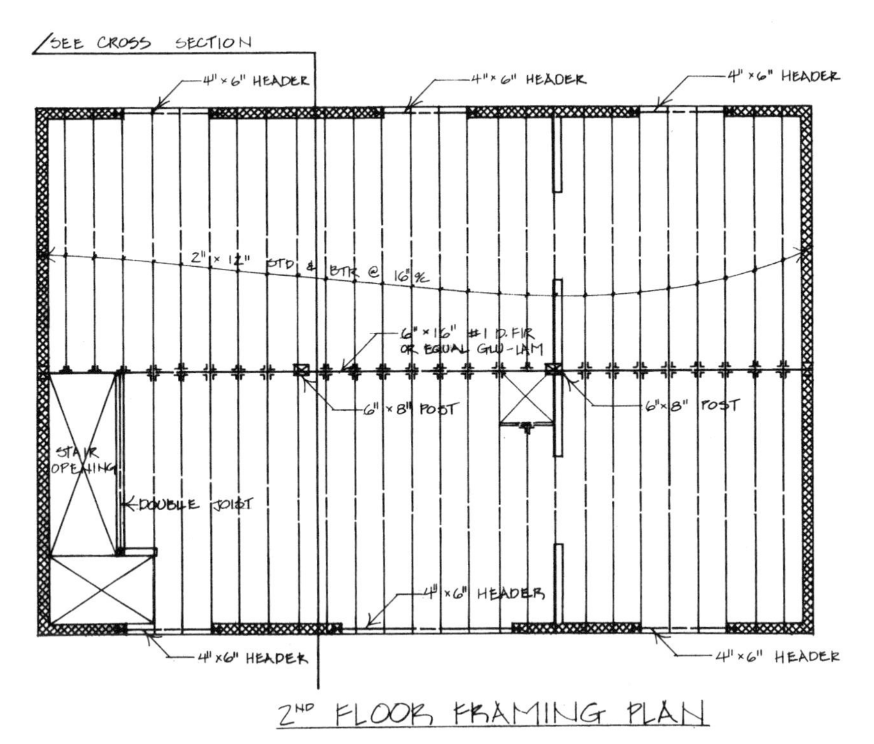


This sturdy floor system is planned for hay storage.

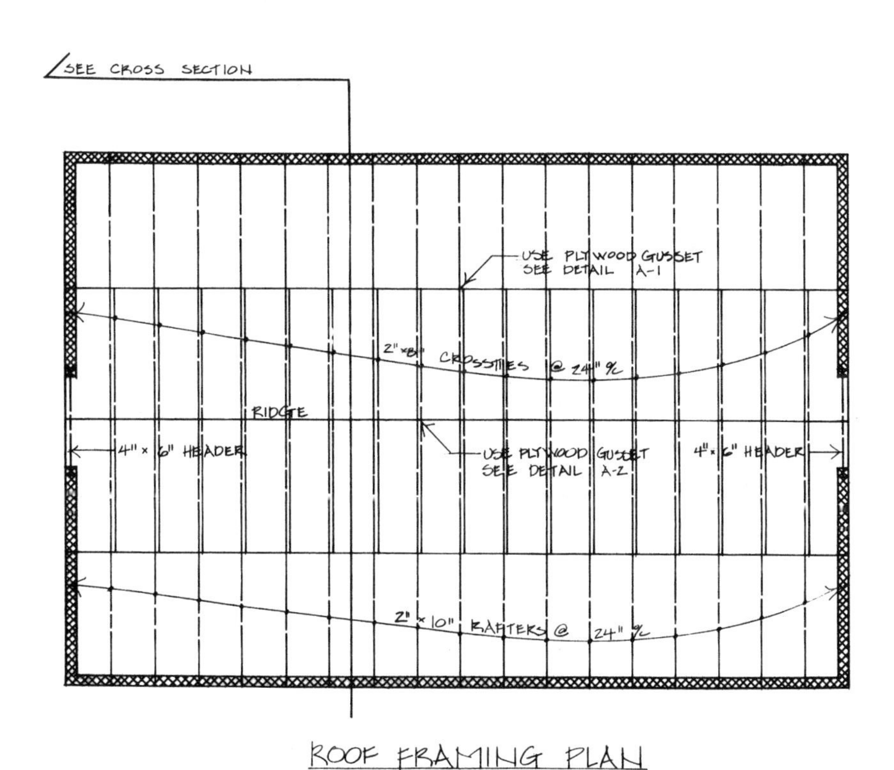


Like our other gambrel barn plans, manufactured trusses can be substituted, if desired.

# The Greenwood

This versatile gambrel barn can be built in a variety of configurations to be used as a barn, a garage, a workshop, or an artist's studio. The optional loft apartment, with a separate entrance, is a popular choice.
The Greenwood is 23' 6" tall.

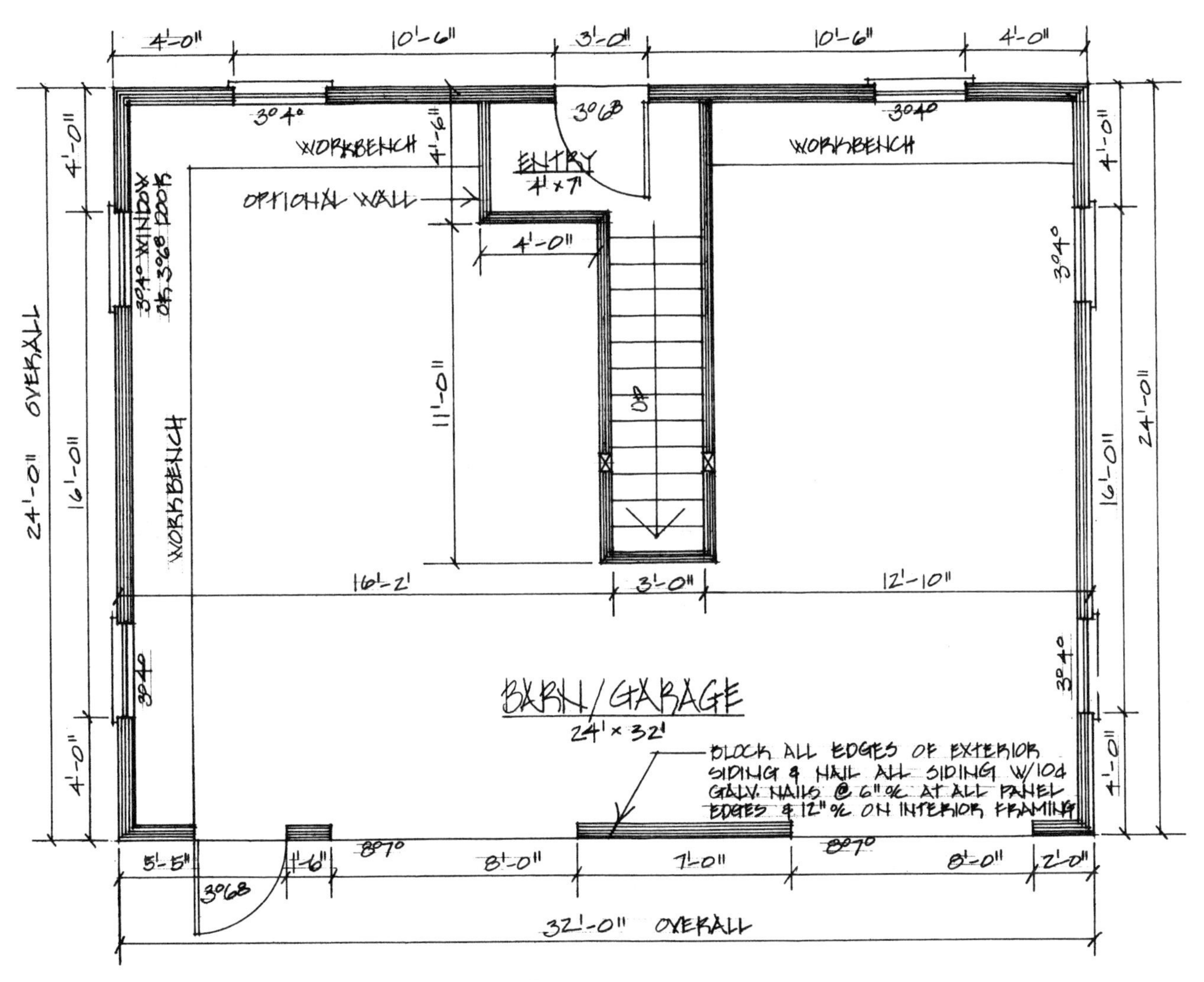


FIRST FLOOR PLAN

The main floor plan shows an enclosed stairwell/entry to allow the loft to be separated from the lower floor. The two doors allow easy access for vehicles or farm equipment. Eliminating the right door would allow room for two large box stalls.

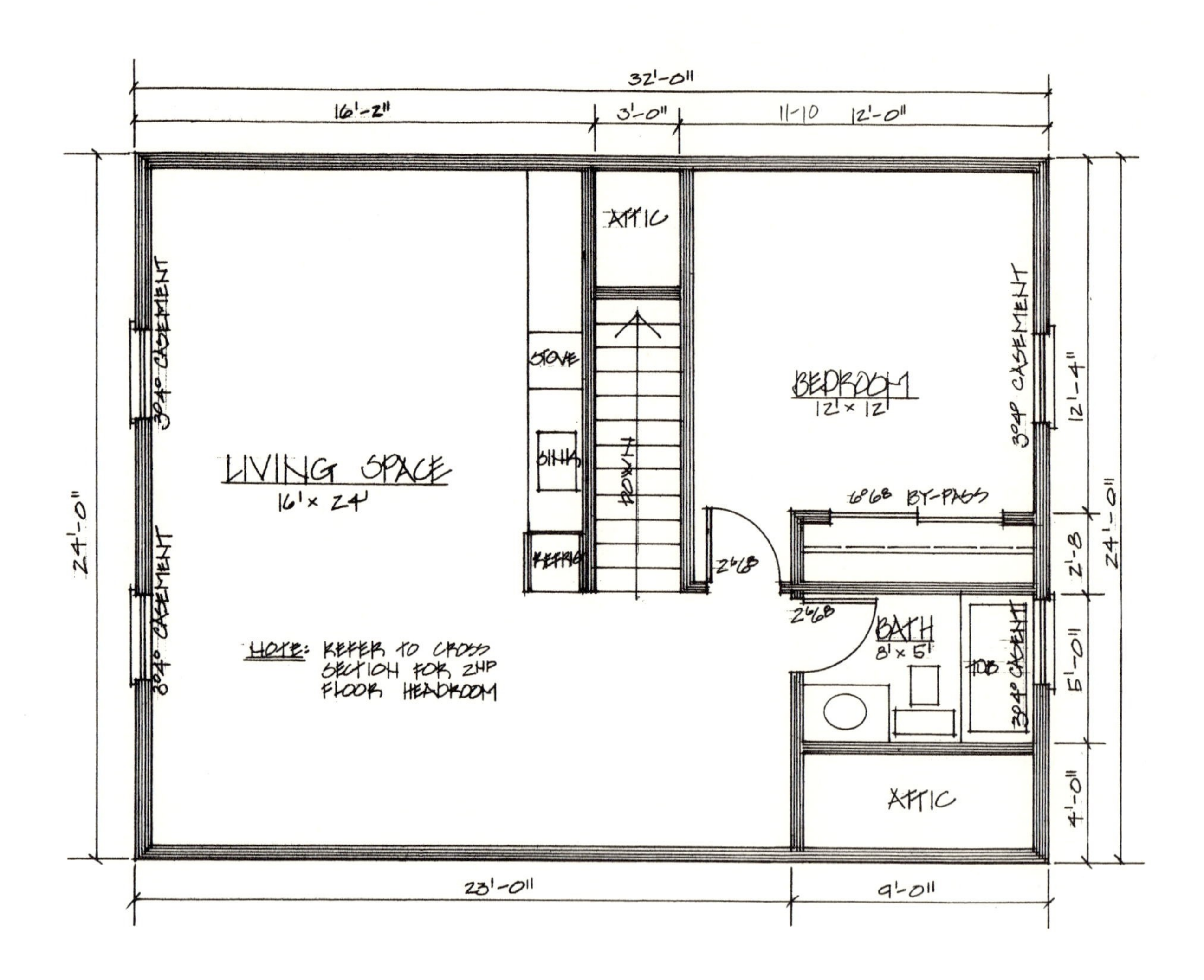


## 2nd Floor Plan

The second-floor apartment features
one bedroom, a full bathroom,
and a large "great room" with an efficiency kitchen.

The large casement windows provide lots of light
and ventilation to both floors of the Greenwood barn.

The "cross-buck" style doors can be site-built
or manufactured doors can be substituted.

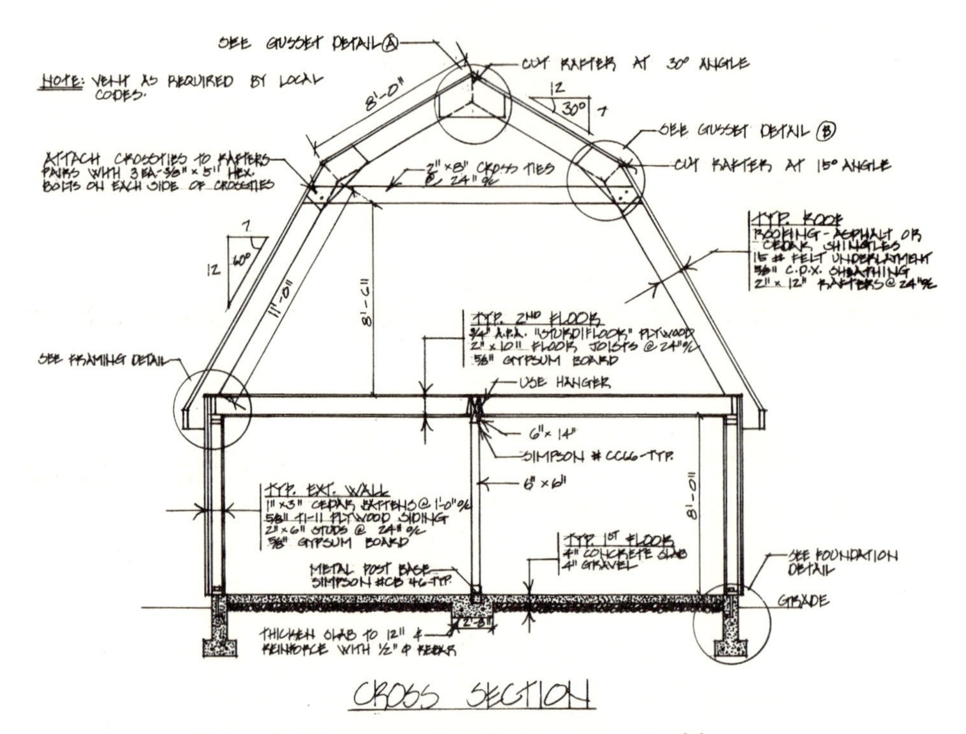


Although this cross-section shows a concrete slab,
the plans for a crawl-space or full basement foundation allow more flexibility
for sloping sites or deep frost lines.

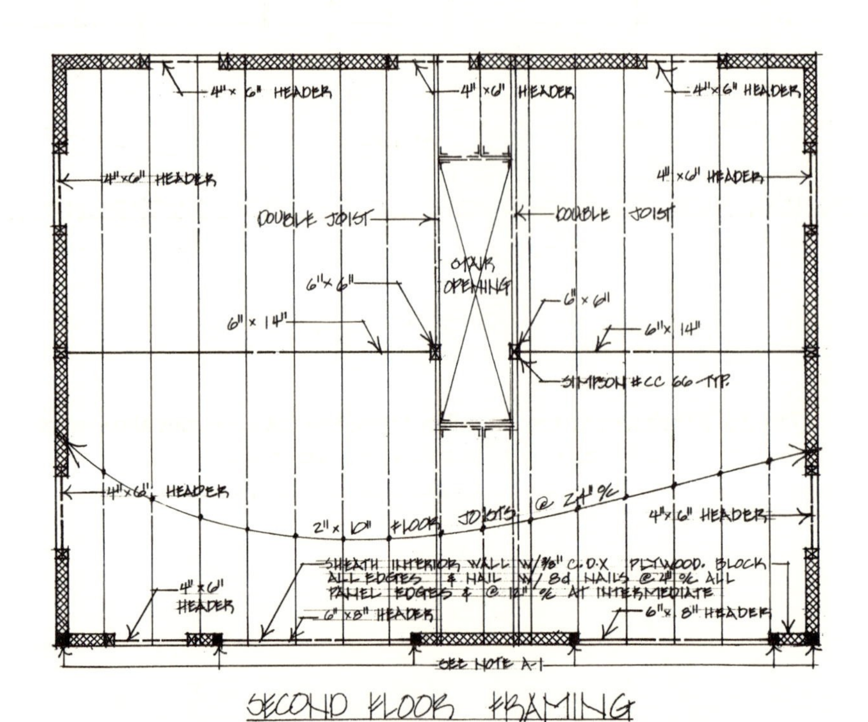


Straight-run stairs are shown here. A turning "U" stair
with a landing, or even a steep "ship's ladder," would permit more flexibility
in the interior layout.

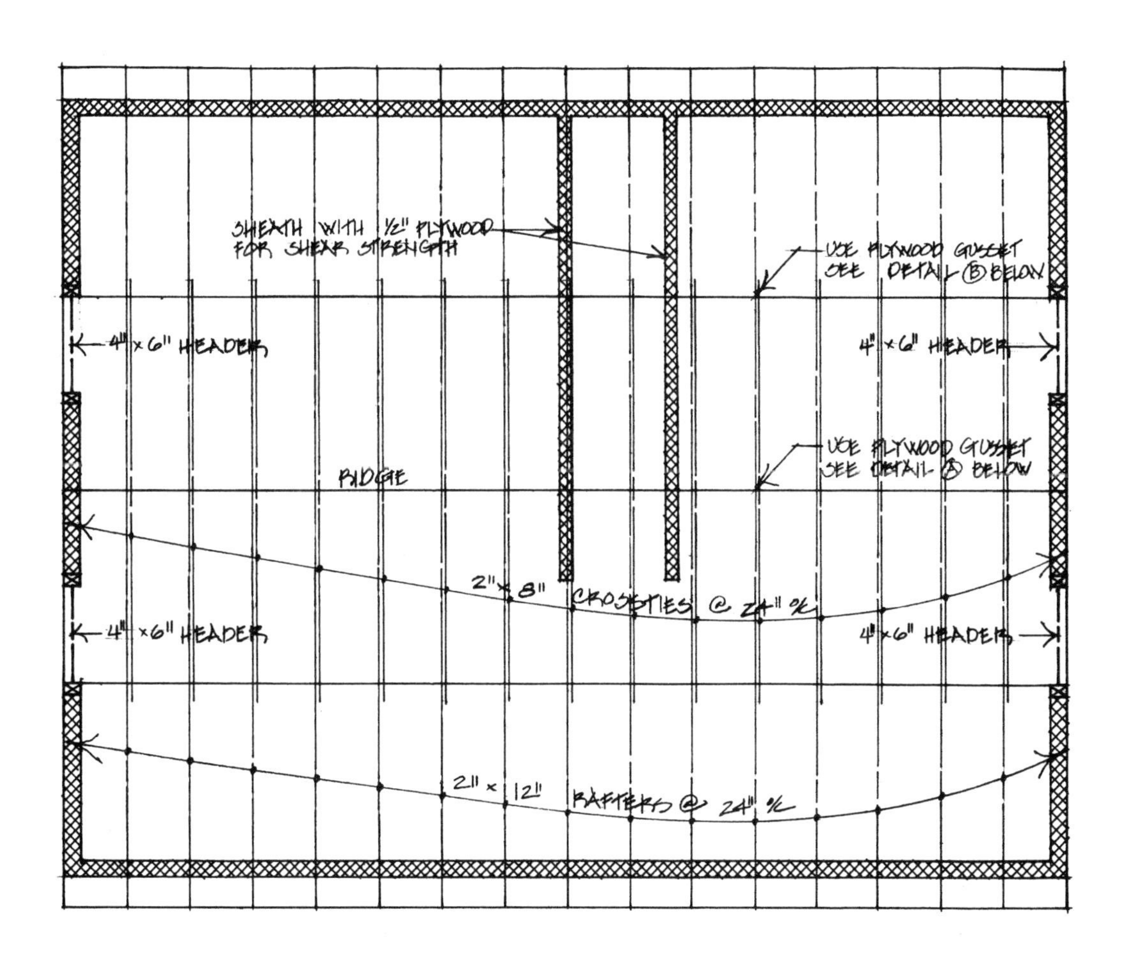


## ROOF FRAMING PLAN

The 2 x 12 rafters and the flat ceiling formed by the cross-ties allow ample room for insulation and ventilation, if the loft is used for finished living space.

# Monitor Roof Barn Plans

## The Lancaster

You can build the Lancaster "monitor" style barn in a variety of layouts because there are only four interior load-bearing posts. This allows you to arrange the interior partitions to fit your specific needs. A 400-square-foot loft with full 8-foot headroom provides room for storage or even a small studio apartment. At the peak, the Lancaster is 21' 3" tall.

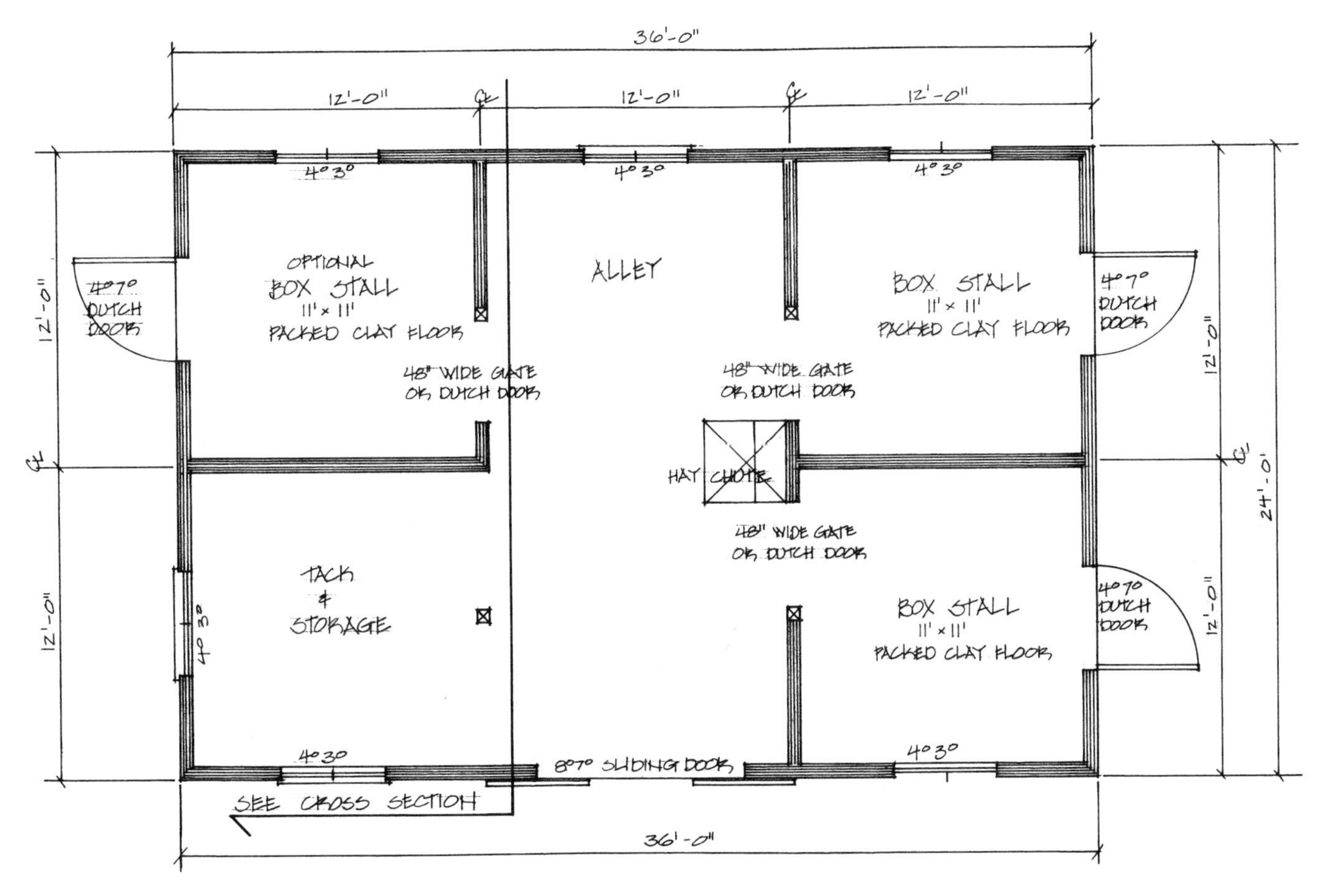


FLOOR PLAN

The center aisle floor plan provides three large box stalls and a generous feed and tack area. Adding another door to the alley allows drive through convenience.

SIDE ELEVATION

Dutch doors provide outside access for each stall, and a large hayloft access makes loading hay easier.

FRONT ELEVATION

Large sliding windows provide lots of light and ventilation to the loft.

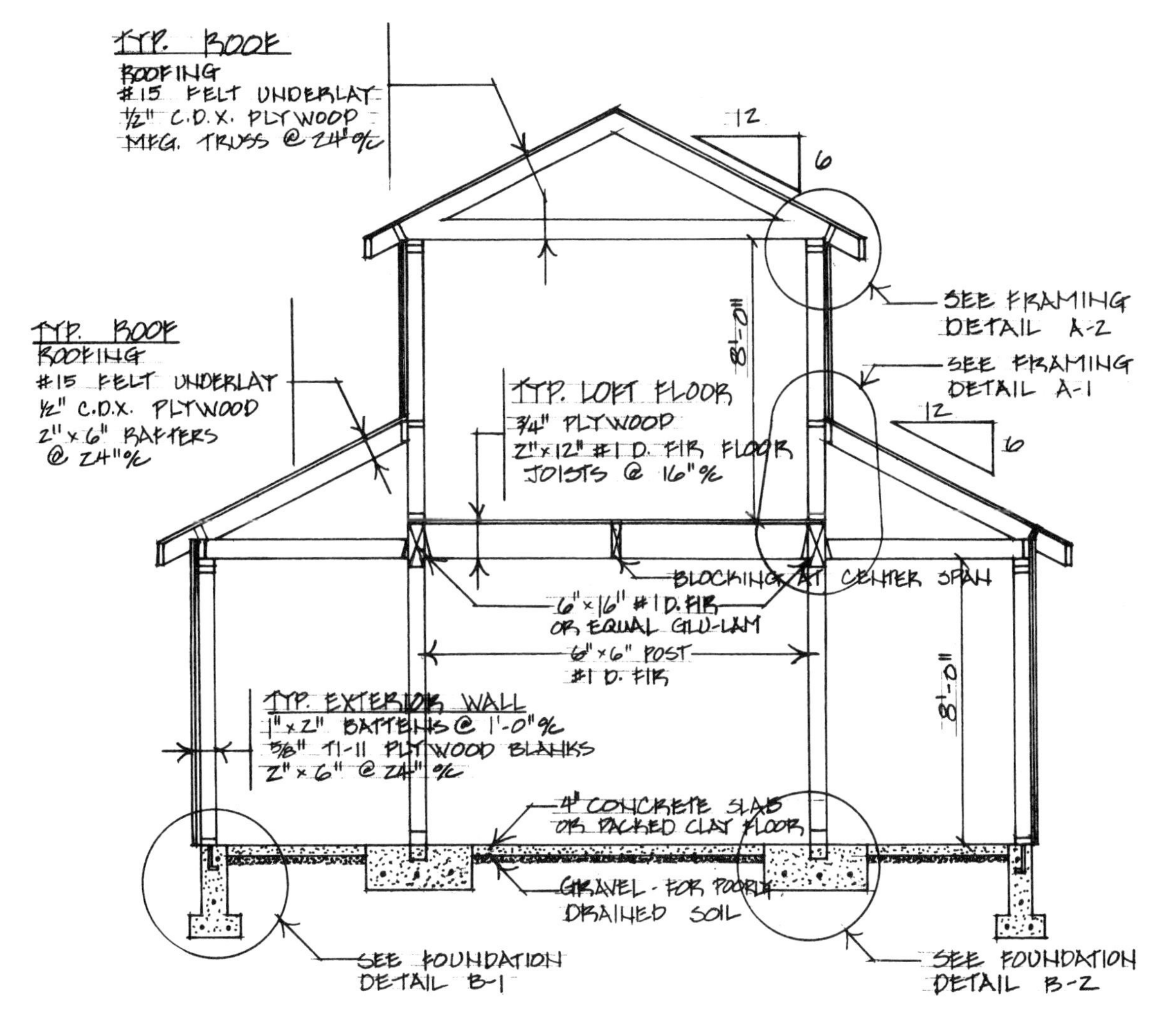


CROSS SECTION

The wall height on the ground floor can be increased to provide extra headroom if required. The loft floor is framed to carry the weight of hay. Smaller joists may be used, if the loft is used for lighter storage.

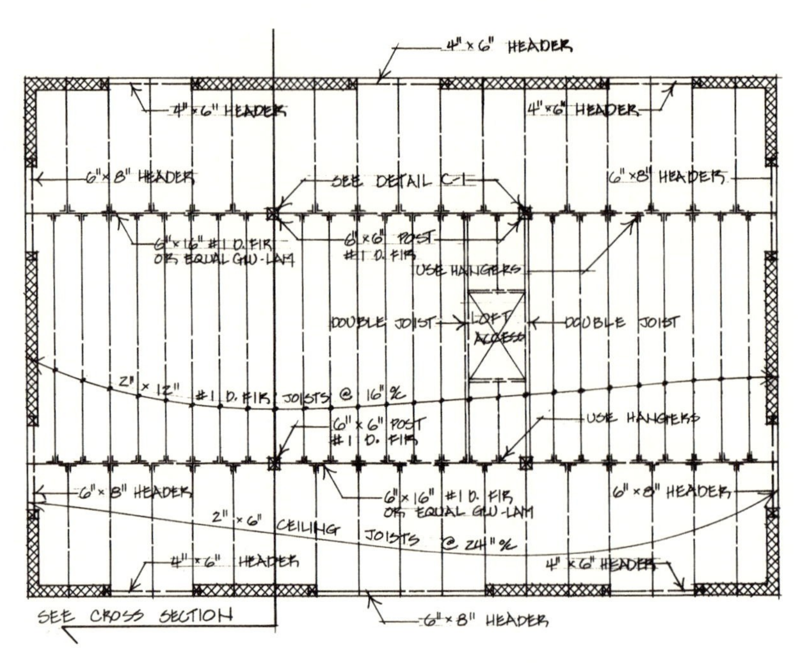


## LOFT FLOOR FRAMING

Manufactured floor joists can be used in place of the 2 x 12s.
A small loft access hatch is shown,
but a standard stairwell can be used also.

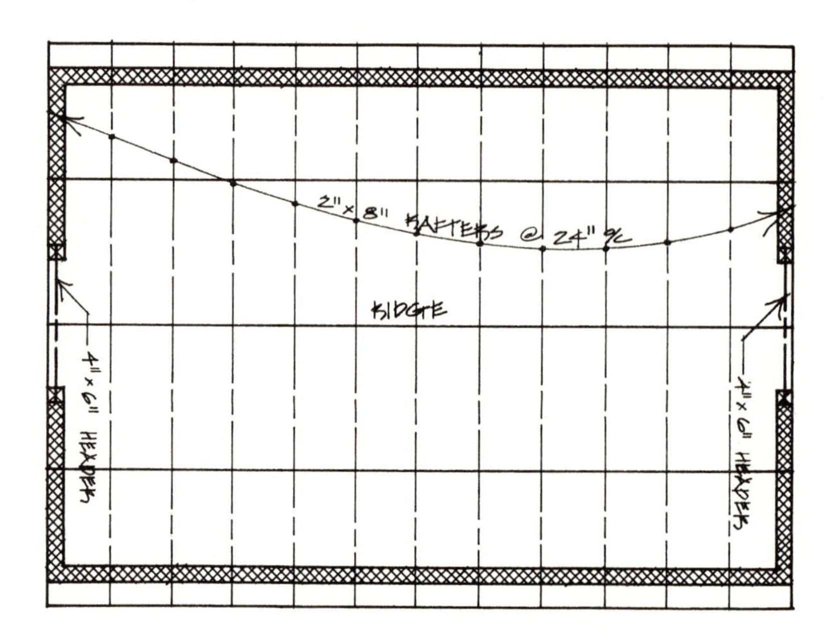


## ROOF FRAMING PLAN

Manufactured trusses are specified for the loft roof for quick and easy framing. The shed roofs over the lower floor can also be framed with manufactured half ("mono") trusses.

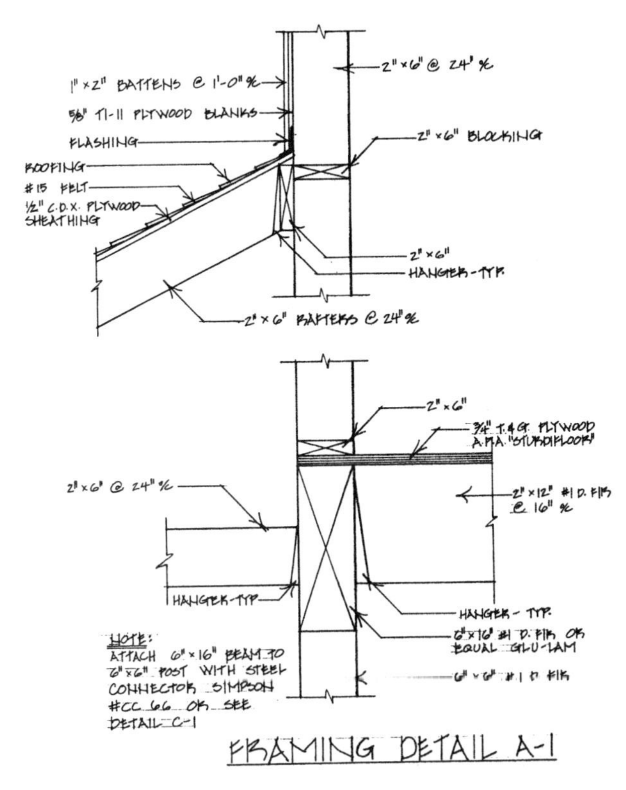


Steel connectors are specified for most wood-to-wood connections to provide maximum strength.

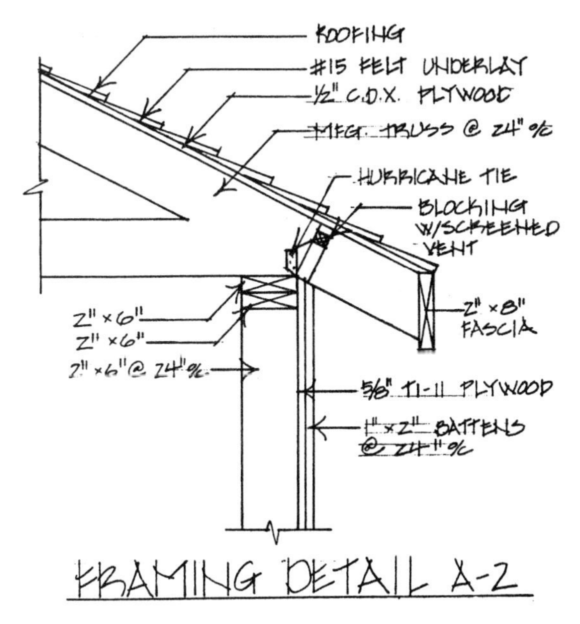


Rough textured plywood with battens serves as both sheathing and siding to keep costs affordable.
Other siding materials can be used if desired.

# The Austin

The Austin features a monitor style roof, and is often called a “Western” style barn. The ground floor has five large box stalls, each with doors on the aisle and the outside, and a large tack and feed room. The 16-foot wide loft runs the full 36-foot length of the barn over the center aisle, and extends over each stall. This makes it easy to drop hay or bedding into each stall. With an outside stair on the end of the barn, the loft can also be a spacious separate apartment or studio. At the ridge, the Austin is 23' 6" high.

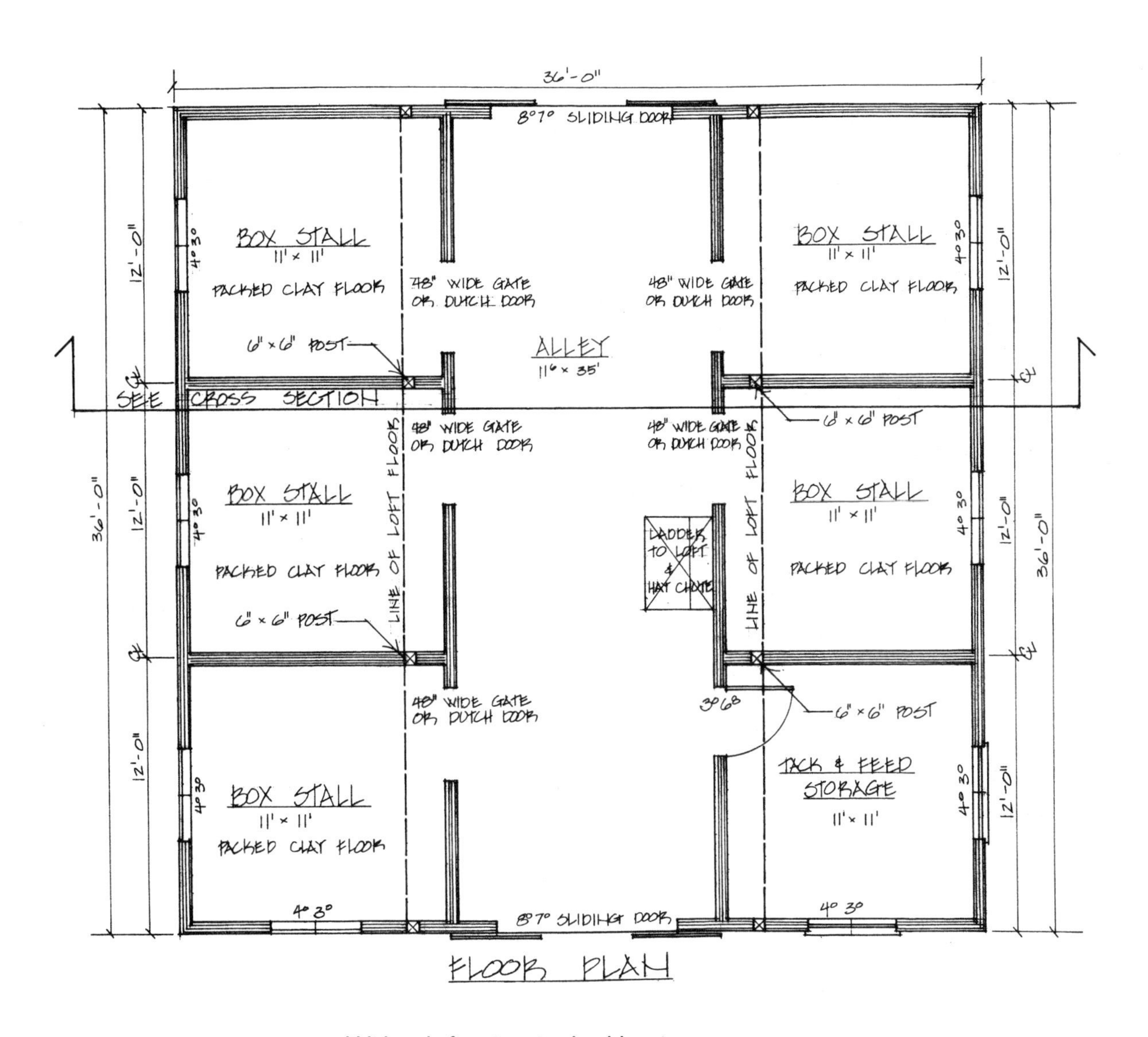


With only four interior load-bearing posts,
it's easy to arrange interior partitions to fit your needs.
With a perimeter concrete foundation wall
for long life, the stalls and alley flooring
can be any material you choose.

REAR ELEVATION

Large loft access doors make hay loading convenient.
If you're using the loft for living or studio space,
windows can be substituted.

SIDE ELEVATION

Evenly-spaced windows brighten the loft, and allow ventilation.

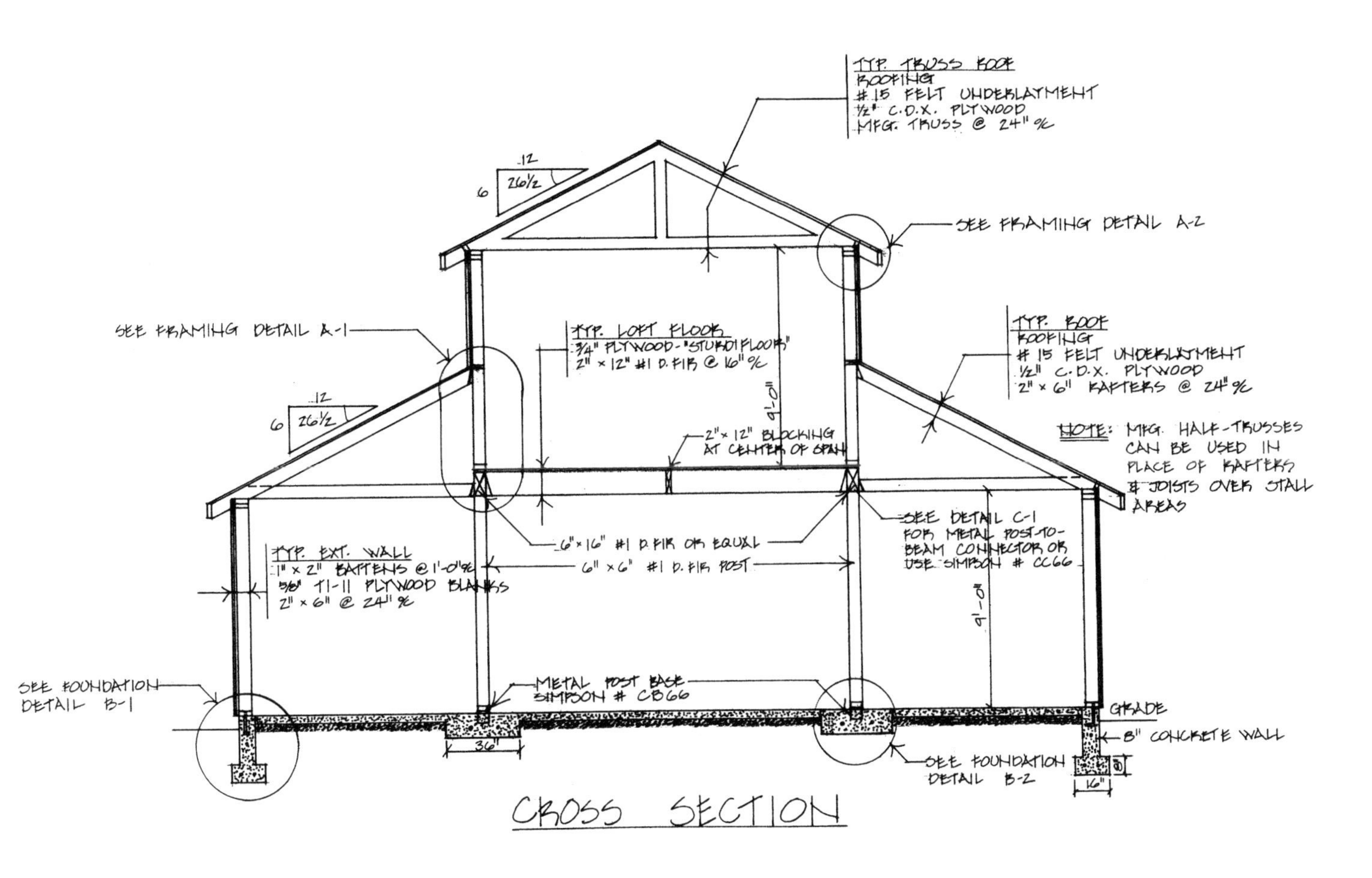


Both the main level and the loft have 9-foot ceilings.

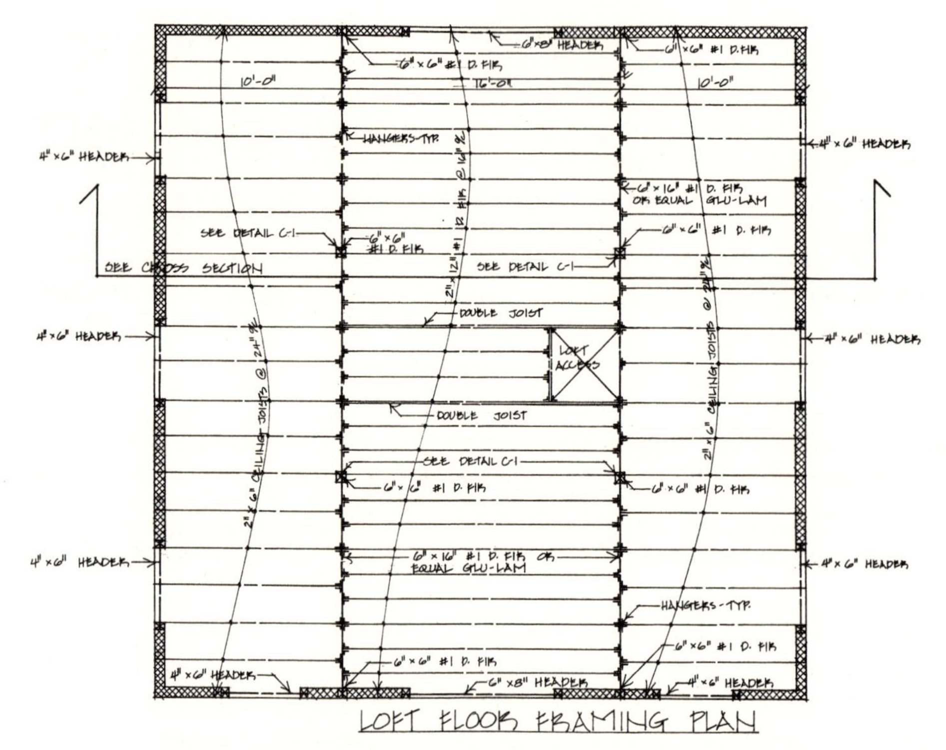


A "ship's ladder" can be used for loft access to save floor space, or a full stairway can be built either inside or outside.

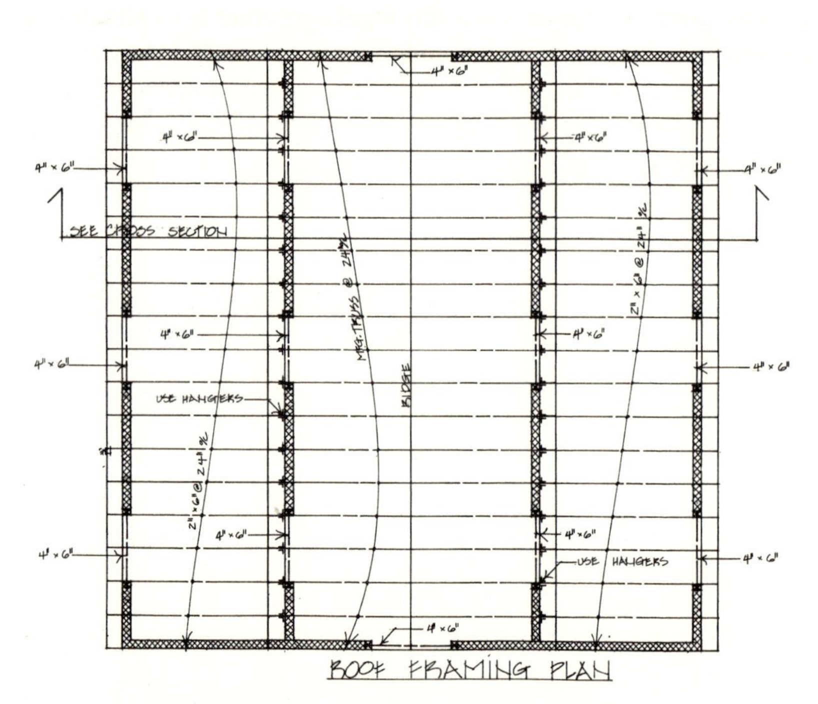


Manufactured trusses, ordered to meet local snow loads, can simplify and speed up the roof framing.

# Construction Forms for Owner-Builders

Most of us hate paperwork, viewing it as a necessary burden. As one contractor put it, "Paperwork never built anything!" You may view these forms in the same way, as a waste of time, but ignore them at your own risk.

A good example is the "selective amnesia" that subcontractors mysteriously develop when billing for changes from the original plans or contract. Without a written change order spelling out the exact details, a verbal change order often becomes a "gravy train' for padded bills and excess charges. Remember— a signed change order protects both the owner and the subcontractor.

The forms that follow in this chapter will help you understand, simplify and control the building process, saving you time and money. The forms also reduce errors, by reminding you to list or schedule, and follow checklists. Items that might have been forgotten on an estimate are not, subs are scheduled on time, and your building project is under *your* control, all with the help of a few forms!

Remember to have your attorney review any legal agreements to ensure that they comply with the laws of your state, and meet your specific needs. Craftsman Books publishes a book/CD titled *Construction Forms and Contracts*, containing 125 forms and contracts that you can customize to use for your building projects. They're listed in the next chapter.

| DESCRIPTION | USE | QUANTITY & SIZE |
|---|---|---|
| Concrete – Footings | Footings & Piers | |
| Concrete – Walls | Foundation Walls | |
| Concrete – Slab | Floor | |
| Reinforcing Steel | Foundation Re-bar | |
| Anchor Bolts | Wall Anchor Bolts | |
| Floor Joists or Trusses | Wood Floor Joists | |
| Floor Sheathing | Wood Floor Sheathing | |
| Support Beams | Wood or Steel Beams | |
| Support Posts | Beam Support Posts | |
| Wall Plates | Wall Top/Bottom Plates | |
| Wall Studs | Wall Framing | |
| Window/Door Headers | Header Beams | |
| Rafters & Cross-Ties | Roof Framing | |
| Manufactured Trusses | Alternate Roof Framing | |
| Roof Sheathing | Roof Sheathing | |
| Roof Underlayment | Underlayment | |
| Roofing | Roofing | |
| Roof Flashing & Vents | Roof Protection | |
| Wall Sheathing | Exterior Walls | |
| Siding | Exterior Walls | |
| Trim Lumber | Wall & Roof Trim | |
| Framing Hardware | Misc. Metal Connectors | |
| Windows | Exterior Windows | |
| Doors | Exterior Doors | |
| Nails | Framing & Finish | |
| Interior Framing | Interior Partitions/Stalls | |
| | | |
| | | |
| | | |
| | | |
| | | |
| | | |
| | | |
| | | |

## CHANGE ORDER

We agree to make the following change:

______________________________________________

______________________________________________

______________________________________________

☐ Increase or ☐ decrease in job cost:

☐ Increase or ☐ decrease in time to completion:

Signature ______________________ Date ______________

Signature ______________________ Date ______________

---

## CHANGE ORDER

We agree to make the following change:

______________________________________________

______________________________________________

______________________________________________

☐ Increase or ☐ decrease in job cost:

☐ Increase or ☐ decrease in time to completion:

Signature ______________________ Date ______________

Signature ______________________ Date ______________

| EXPENSE | SCHEDULE | START | FINISH |
|---|---|---|---|
| Temporary Power | | | |
| Building Permits | | | |
| Utility Easements | | | |
| Clearing/Excavation | | | |
| Foundation | | | |
| Buried Plumbing | | | |
| Concrete Slab | | | |
| Backfill Foundation | | | |
| Shell Framing | | | |
| Rough-in Plumbing | | | |
| Rough-in Electrical | | | |
| Masonry | | | |
| Roofing | | | |
| Gutters | | | |
| Exterior Doors | | | |
| Exterior Windows | | | |
| Siding/Trim | | | |
| Exterior Paint/Stain | | | |
| Final Grading | | | |
| Insulation | | | |
| Interior Walls/Stalls | | | |
| Interior Floors | | | |
| Plumbing Fixtures | | | |
| Electrical Fixtures | | | |
| Move-In! | | | |

# CONSTRUCTION COST SCHEDULE

| EXPENSE | ESTIMATE | ACTUAL COST |
|---|---|---|
| Cabinets | | |
| Carpentry, Finish | | |
| Carpentry, Framing | | |
| Concrete Flatwork | | |
| Contingency Funds | | |
| Doors & Windows | | |
| Drywall | | |
| Electrical | | |
| Excavation | | |
| Fencing & Gates | | |
| Foundation | | |
| Gutters | | |
| Flooring | | |
| Heating System | | |
| Insurance | | |
| Landscaping | | |
| Loan Costs | | |
| Lumber, Finish | | |
| Lumber, Framing | | |
| Masonry | | |
| Paint/Stain | | |
| Paving | | |
| Permits | | |
| Plans | | |
| Plumbing | | |
| Roofing | | |
| Sand & Gravel | | |
| Siding & Trim | | |
| Stall Components | | |
| Utilities | | |
| Ventilation System | | |
| Misc. Labor | | |
| Misc. Materials | | |
| TOTAL COST | | |

**Excavation**
Assumed soil bearing capacity of 1,500 p.s.i., or as required by local code.
Clear building site of all vegetation, rocks and stumps and excavate to undisturbed soil.

**Foundation**
Concrete mix: 2500 p.s.i. minimum.
Concrete slab: minimum 4" thickness, reinforced with 6 x 6 #10 wire mesh.
Sills: pressure-treated foundation grade.
Termite protection as required by local building codes.
Footing drains: 4" drain in gravel bed, where conditions require.
Footing depth: Place footing below local frost line.
Embedded structural posts to be A.W.P.A. rated for ground contact.

**Carpentry**
All framing to be plumb, level and square, and securely nailed, stapled or bolted to meet building code requirements.

**Floor framing**
All wood joists and beams to be minimum 1,200 p.s.i. lumber bending strength, unless otherwise noted on plans. Bridging, beam and joist hangars, anchor bolts and post anchors as required by local building codes.
Plywood floors to be minimum 3/4" tongue and groove graded "Sturdifloor"™ or underlayment.

**Exterior walls**
Wall studs to be standard or better grade.
Building paper to be 15# felt or "Tyvek"™.
Plywood siding or sheathing to be 1/2" minimum, nailed with 7d galvanized nails, 6" o.c. at panel edges and 10" o.c. intermediate. Match siding on adjacent buildings where appropriate.

**Roof framing**
Rafters: lumber to be 1,200 p.s.i. minimum.
Roof sheathing: 1/2" CDX or equal.
Ply-clips to be used at the panel edges between rafters or trusses.
Use 1/2" CCX or 5/8" APA siding at exposed soffits and gable ends.
Nailing schedule: 7d nails at 6" o.c. at panel edges, and at 10' o.c. intermediate.

**Roofing**
Roofing material and installation to meet or exceed building codes.

**Insulation**
Type of material:____________________

Ceiling insulation R-value:______________

Wall insulation R-value:________________

Floor insulation R-value:_______________

**Interior finish carpentry**
Trim:____________________________

Doors:___________________________
Wrap all treated wood exposed to animals with untreated wood or metal for protection.

**Utilities**
Provide electrical service, water supply and sewage disposal per local codes.

**Finish grading**
Provide positive drainage for water away from buildings on all sides.

**Exterior finish**
Exterior siding and trim to be stained or painted with:______________________

**Ventilation**
As required by local conditions.

# Owner-Builder Resources and Cupola Plans

As you begin planning your new barn, take the time to explore some of these helpful resources. Rather than list addresses and phone numbers, I've listed a Web site for each resource, so you can access the information more quickly and easily. Even better, many of the sites offer information that can be downloaded at no cost, rather than paying for a printed version.

If you don't have access to the Internet, sit down at a friend's computer for a while. You'll learn how to access Web sites in just a few minutes. Don't have any friends with computers? Go to your local public library, where you'll find not only the computers to search the World Wide Web, but friendly, patient librarians who are happy to show you how.

New Web sites are being created every day, so don't limit yourself to the ones I've listed in this chapter! The best way to find new resources is to do a "Web search", using one of the many search engines available. My personal favorite is Google.com for their speedy and thorough searches. For example, typing in the keywords "barn plans" will lead you to almost every Web site worth looking at.

## More barn plans

In 1999, architect Donald Berg opened aBetterPlan.com as a source for hard-to-find plans, and resources for building barns, garages, sheds, outbuildings and simple country homes. Since then, it's grown into one of the most popular building Web sites on the Internet.

You should be able to find plans for your perfect small barn, garage, or outbuilding from one of dozens of architects and designers. You'll also find resources for pole barn construction, post and beam kits, antique barns, and custom barn designs.

You'll find help in planning your property and links to specialists who offer advice and guidebooks on horse farm planning, building codes and country landscaping. There are also sources for cupolas, weathervanes, stable equipment and accessories for your new barns. Start your search at www.aBetterPlan.com.

For over 20 years, Homestead Design has been a source for building plans drawn with the owner-builder in mind. Their Web site features plans for traditional designs of garden sheds, barns, stables, garages and compact, affordable country homes. You've seen 12 of the plans in this book; take a look at the rest at www.homesteaddesign.com.

BGS Plan Company offers hundreds of plans for barns, garages, and other agricultural buildings. Because they are in earthquake country, their plans reflect those special requirements, and all plans include engineering calculations. Because the plans are stamped by an engineer, plan prices are expensive. View their catalog online at www.bgsplanco.com.

At the other end of the price spectrum, you'll find dozens of free, downloadable plans at the Midwest Plan Service. MWPS is an organization of agricultural engineers from 12 Land Grant universities located in the Midwest states, such as Illinois, Iowa and Wisconsin. The free plans range from hay barns to horse barns, with even a small farm home or two. You can see the plans at their Web site, www.mwpshq.org. County extension agents in most states have a looseleaf binder with all the plans available for copying at no charge.

The Canadian equivalent of MWPS is the Canada Plan Service, also a network of agricultural engineers, who have developed several excellent plans that can be downloaded free at their Web site. You can also order full-size plans from one of the resources listed, even if you are not a Canadian resident. My favorite is Plan 8203, a two-story gambrel horse barn. This plan also details an economical and easy-to-fabricate stall door using readily available materials. You'll find the plans at www.cps.gov.on.ca.

## Barn components

**Country Manufacturing** fabricates a wide variety of barn components to help you complete your barn. They have modular stalls, stall grills and doors, door guards and feeders, and Dutch door kits. You can purchase just the components you need, or a complete door or stall. Visit their Web site at www.countrymfg.com.

It's obvious when you find **cupola.com** that Howard Partridge is fascinated by cupolas. Here you can learn how to size a cupola, view galleries of historic cupolas, and find links for ready-made cupolas, kits and plans. Start by clicking on "site index" on the home page, then click on "Cupola F.A.Q." where you can find a list of dozens of cupola builders, plan sources, and related sites. www.cupola.com.

**Double L Group** manufactures a simple do-it-yourself stall kit, with all the metal work and hardware you need, and complete instructions for assembly. The lumber needed can be bought at your local lumberyard. The metal parts are all made from Galvalume™, which is very durable and long-lasting. You can see the kits at www.doublel.com.

**HTCadd.com** has designed plans for a variety of garden structures, such as gazebos, arbors, covered bridges and cupolas. Their 26 fanciful cupola designs, one for each letter of the alphabet, are reasonably priced and quite unique. If you want to have the most eye-catching cupola in your neighborhood, look here for help! www.HTCadd.com.

**Linear Rubber Products** makes natural rubber stall mats that are non-porous and can be installed over any surface, even dirt. They claim that the reduced costs of bedding can pay for the mats in two years. See the mats at www.rubbermats.com.

**Lumber Link** is an engineered system that allows you to erect a post and beam structure without using preservative-treated posts, a conventional foundation or roof trusses. The metal sockets allow a do-it-yourselfer to build faster, easier and cheaper, with clear spans up to 30 feet in gable, gambrel and clerestory designs. See the possibilities at www.socketsystems.com.

**New England Cupola and Weathervane** make cupolas in many styles, such as “Cape Cod” and “Nantucket”, and in several sizes. If you don’t find a stock size and style, custom cupolas are their specialty. Visit them at www.newenglandcupola.com.

**National Manufacturing** makes one of the most complete lines of sliding door hardware. Their box and round track, hangars, rollers and guides are available in just about any weight capacity you might need. You’ll need to order through a local lumberyard or home center, but you can view their on-line catalog at www.natman.com. Click on “hangars and rail” on the home page menu to find the hardware.

**RAMMfence** makes, in addition to fencing, stall kits with standard tubular or welded grills and solid stall panels. Their Pro-Tek stall kits are shipped with instructions, and you supply the lumber. Their on-line stall selection guide makes it easy to choose the best system for your needs. View it at www.rammfence.com.

**Werner Ladder** makes two styles of pull-down folding access ladders. One is a heavy-duty aluminum ladder, the other is wood. If you plan to use your barn loft only for limited storage, a space-saving access ladder might be a better choice than a permanent staircase. Werner ladders, or other comparable brands, are available at most lumberyards and home centers. To see the Werner attic access ladders, go to www.wernerladder.com.

**Woodstar Products** fabricates barn components and accessories, including stalls, grills, portable stalls, miniature stalls, doors and even barn cupolas. You can buy individual components, such as U-channels for stall walls, door hardware and panels, or finished products. View their on-line catalog at www.wdstar.com.

**W.W. Grainger** is a national industrial supplier that carries a wide range of ventilators. You can choose from automatic power ventilators, gable-end ventilator fans, whole-building fans or roof-mounted attic fans. All can be controlled by a thermostat, humidistat or timer. If your building has no electricity, or you don't want an electric fan, check out their "turbine ventilators", designed to remove hot air in summer and moist air in winter. The turbines rotate with a passing breeze, creating a strong upward draft to remove inside air. Their enormous on-line catalog also includes the Stanley line of sliding barn door hardware. Their web site is at www.grainger.com.

## Books

The books listed here are available at most libraries, either on the shelf or through an inter-library loan. Since they all are available in paperback for under $20 each, I would recommend that you purchase them for your own library. These are the kind of books that you will want to have close at hand while you're building. Book in one hand, hammer in the other, you'll find the building goes faster, with fewer mistakes with these pros to help you. For one-stop book shopping, try www.amazon.com.

***Building a Multi-Use Barn,*** by John D. Wagner. If you could only have one book to guide you through the actual construction of a barn, this would be it. Hundreds of detailed photos, illustrations and photographs guide you step-by-step through every phase of barn building, from setting up foundation forms to wiring a light fixture.

***House Framing*** is another great book by John D. Wagner, with over 400 drawings to make each phase of framing crystal clear. It's especially helpful with roof framing, such as cutting compound angles for dormer rafters.

***Working Alone,*** by Jack Carroll. This unique book offers do-it-yourselfers a multitude of ways to get by with just one pair of hands—safely. Backyard builders who work alone, often by necessity, will find this book full of clever techniques to solve common problems safely and efficiently.

**Craftsman Book Company** has one of the most complete selections of construction books available. From cost estimating guides to framing manuals to construction law, they cover it all. View their on-line catalog at www.craftsman-book.com.

## Government resources

**The Department of Housing and Urban Development (HUD)** has encouraged the development of affordable building techniques for many years. One of the most interesting is called the "Frost-Protected Shallow Foundation" (FPSF), developed many years ago in the Scandinavian countries and used in over 1 million homes. One builder in the Midwest, using the FPSF instead of a conventional deep foundation wall, was able to reduce the foundation cost by over $3,000 on a single home. You can download the FPSF building guide free at the HUD Web site, as well as many other useful publications. Go to www.huduser.org, then click on "publications", then click on "building technology".

**NRAES,** a service of USDA Cooperative Extension and 14 Land-Grant colleges in the Northeast, publishes an extensive list of booklets and videos aimed at the farm community. From fencing to greenhouse construction, there's something for almost everyone. Of particular interest to barn builders is the "Post-Frame Building Handbook", #NRAES-1, a primer on designing and building pole-frame buildings. Another essential publication for horse owners is the "Horse Housing and Equipment Handbook", #MWPS-15. You can see the entire catalog at www.nraes.org. On the home page, click on "guide to great publications".

**Cooperative Extension,** a part of the U.S. Department of Agriculture, has an agent in every county in the U.S. They are there to serve the general public, so if you have questions about animals, barns, crops or any agricultural topic, call or visit. They work closely with each state's Land-Grant college, so you can tap experts on almost any topic if they don't have the answers themselves.

## Legal resources

Craftsman Book company, mentioned earlier in this chapter, publishes an excellent book titled ***Contractor's Plain-English Legal Guide.*** A CD-ROM is included with the book that has over 100 legal forms. You can download several of the forms free, at www.costbook.com. Click on "Download free legal forms".

**NOLO** is an organization that has helped people handle their own everyday legal matters for almost 30 years. Their Web site is packed with articles on almost any legal topic, including many related to construction, and links to other helpful Web sites. They also publish reliable plain-English books, software and legal forms that you can buy or download from the Web site. One area where owner-builders often run afoul of various government agencies is hiring independent contractors. NOLO publishes an excellent guide, *How to Safely and Legally Hire Independent Contractors.* Visit NOLO at www.nolo.com.

## Trade associations

**APA – The Engineered Wood Association** publishes dozens of helpful booklets that can show you how to build a better barn. One example is ***Sturd-I-Frames for Narrow Wall Bracing.*** Often it's necessary to place a door opening closer than 4 feet to a corner, which reduces the ability of the building to stand up to the lateral forces of winds and earthquakes. The APA has developed, and tested, a framing system that allows walls as narrow as 16 inches to provide the code-required strength and stiffness. If you live in an area where wall bracing requirements are enforced, you have a choice: pay an engineer several hundred dollars to design a solution, or download this free publication! To access this, and all other APA free and low-cost publications, go to www.apawood.org. Click on "Search our publications database" on the home page, then click on the topic "residential construction."

**The American Wood Council** provides wood design and construction information for both homeowners and construction professionals. They have a free manual available for download called "Details for Conventional Wood Frame Construction". It's full of helpful building tips, over 60 illustrations of framing details, and tables. To get the free manual, go to www.awc.org. Click on "Publications", then "Free download library". The manual is #WCD1.

**The WWPA** is a lumber trade association that publishes information, such as span tables and other design and engineering information on a variety of lumber species, from Douglas fir to Southern pine. One of the most useful resources at their Web site is a series of digital span tables. Using the on-line span tables, you can find spans for any species of lumber for most combinations of floor, ceiling and roof loads. A pull-down menu for floor joists, ceiling joists and roof rafters lets you select the exact loads appropriate to your area and local codes, and then shows the allowable span for the load and species of wood. To access this useful tool, go to www.wwpa.org. Click on "Technical Guide", then "spans".

# The "Homestead" Cupola Plans

This cupola was designed to be an easy-to-build and affordable alternative to the expensive cupolas available for sale. Instead of costing several hundred dollars, the Homestead cupola uses "stock" materials such as pre-fab louver vents from the lumberyard, and scraps from the construction of your barn to keep the cost low. The prototype cost under $100, and was built and installed in 6 hours.

Rather than using hip rafters, with their complicated compound angle cuts, a simple center post, bevel cut to match the roof pitch, provides support for the peak, and a sturdy base for an optional weathervane.

## How big should a cupola be?

Most cupolas look best when they are about 1/12th the length of the roof where they sit. For example, a 24-foot-long barn roof would use a 24-inch-square cupola. If your roof is longer than 30 feet, you can use one large or two or more smaller cupolas. Using several smaller cupolas provides balanced ventilation for the barn along the ridge, and the smaller cupolas are easier to hoist in place safely.

By the time you've framed the shell of your building, there should be a decent scrap pile to use for cupola parts. The 5/8 inch plywood used for the exterior barn walls can be used for the cupola walls as-is, or sided with other materials. Scraps of 3/4-inch plywood from the loft floor can be used for the cupola roof sheathing.

### Assembling the cupola box

Start construction of your cupola by making a square plywood box in the size you've chosen, and at least a foot taller than the vents you've chosen. Corner studs can be either 2 x 2 or 2 x 4 scraps from your barn construction. Although screws are shown attaching the corners, for increased strength, nailing is O.K.

Next, after the plywood box is assembled, cut out the bottom notch on two sides to match the pitch of the roof where the cupola will be mounted. The angle cut at the base of the cupola should match the slope of the roof. After you've made the angle cuts, cut out the holes for the louvered vents that will be installed.

If you're on a tight budget, plastic or metal louver vents are economical. Wood looks best, and most lumberyards stock, or can order, cedar or redwood louver vents in a variety of sizes. Run a bead of exterior caulk around the edge of each opening before installing the vents to ensure a weather-tight seal.

The corner trim can be 1 x 3 or 1 x 4 boards. If your cupola is smaller than 30 inches, use 1 x 3's. Stop the corner boards 1 inch from the top of the plywood box. This allows the cupola roof cap to overhang the box for a good weather seal.

### Assembling the cupola roof

To simplify the roof framing, the plywood roof sheathing is 3/4-inch, thicker than normal roof sheathing, so it can easily span the distance from the center 4 x 4 post to the outer frame without the usual hip rafters.

Start by ripping the bevel cut on the top of the 2 x 4's that make up the outer frame. The angle should be the same as the roof slope where the cupola will be installed. The 4 x 4 center post is also beveled on all four sides to match the roof slope. Notch the 2 x 4 post supports to allow the roof assembly to overlap the cupola box, as shown in the drawings.

Assemble the roof system as shown in the drawings. After the roof system is assembled, install the roofing to match the building. Depending on the weight, you may want to take the two individual cupola assemblies (the box and the roof cap) up on the roof for installation, rather than completely assembling the cupola on the ground first.

Cut out the hole in the roof, and attach the cupola, using metal ties and screws. Install flashing on all four sides to provide a weather seal.

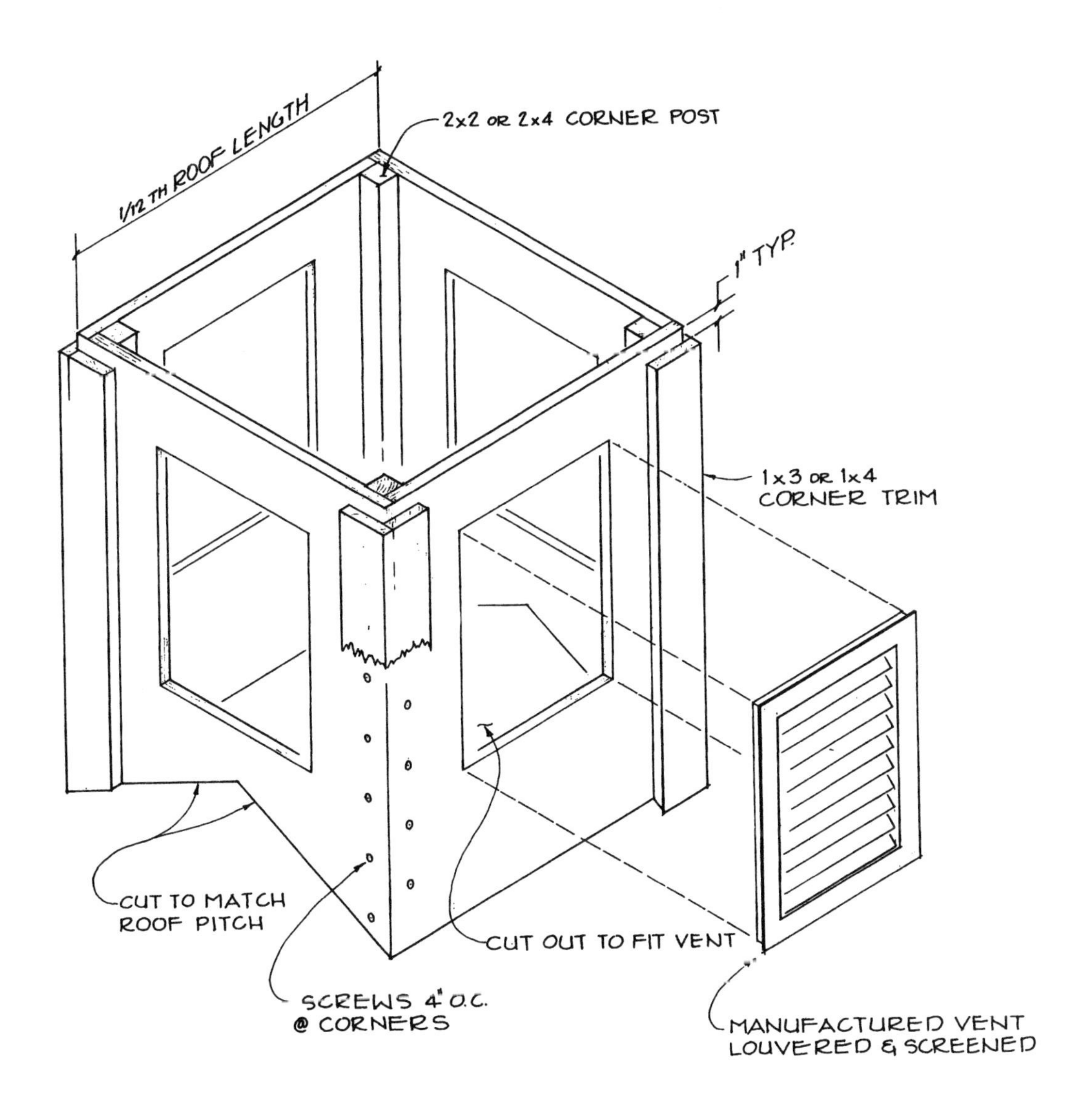

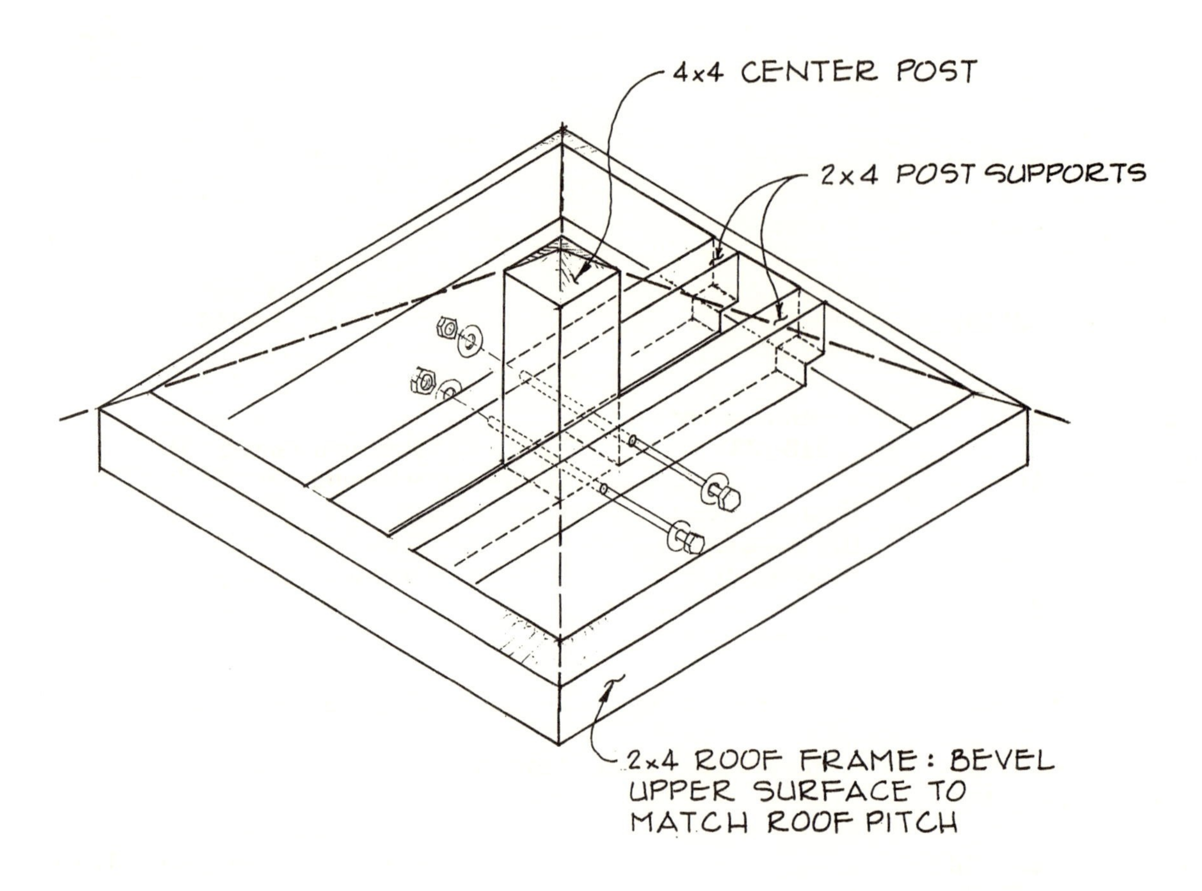
4x4 CENTER POST
2x4 POST SUPPORTS
2x4 ROOF FRAME: BEVEL
UPPER SURFACE TO
MATCH ROOF PITCH

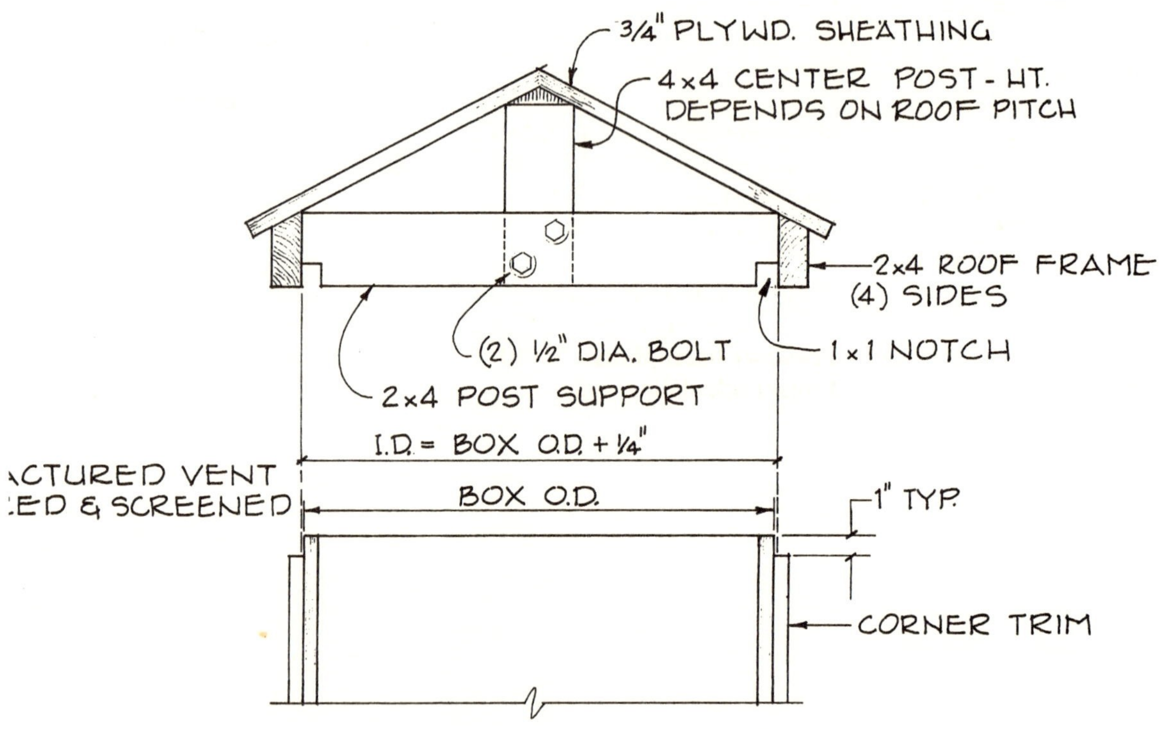
3/4" PLYWD. SHEATHING
4x4 CENTER POST - HT.
DEPENDS ON ROOF PITCH
2x4 ROOF FRAME
(4) SIDES
(2) 1/2" DIA. BOLT
1x1 NOTCH
2x4 POST SUPPORT
I.D. = BOX O.D. + 1/4"
BOX O.D.
1" TYP.
CORNER TRIM

# Index

## RUSH ORDER FORM

**FAX ORDERS:** (360) 385-9983.
Send this form.

**TELEPHONE ORDERS:** Call (360) 385-9983
to order plans or books using your credit card.
Our hours are 10 a.m. to 3 p.m. Pacific Time.

**INTERNET ORDERS:** www.homesteaddesign.com
Order on our secure server.

**POSTAL ORDERS:**
Homestead Design
P.O. Box 2010
Port Townsend, WA 98368

## PRICE LIST

**All barn plans:** $39.95 per set. (Expanded plans, drawn to full architectural scale on 11"x17" sheets, includes all drawings shown in this book, plus additional elevations, foundation plans, all floor plan variations, structural detail drawings, specifications and a complete materials list)
**Extra sets** of the same plan: $9.95 per extra set.
**Extra copies of this book,** *Small Barn Plans for Owner-Builders:* $19.95
**Shipping:** $4.00 for first book or plan, $2.00 for each additional item.

| Name of Plan or Book | Quantity | Price |
|---|---|---|
| | | |
| | | |
| | | |
| | *Shipping* | |
| | *8.2% Washington State Sales Tax (if applicable)* | |
| | **TOTAL** | |

Name: ______________________________

Address: ______________________________

City: ____________________ State: __________ Zip: __________

Payment: ❑ Check or Money Order ❑ Visa ❑ Mastercard

Card Number: ____________________ Expiration Date: __________

Daytime Phone Number: ____________________ E-Mail: ____________________